Grant Powers

Historical Sketches of the Discovery, Settlement and Progress of Events in the Coos Country and Vicinity

Grant Powers

Historical Sketches of the Discovery, Settlement and Progress of Events in the Coos Country and Vicinity

ISBN/EAN: 9783337236274

Printed in Europe, USA, Canada, Australia, Japan

Cover: Foto ©ninafisch / pixelio.de

More available books at **www.hansebooks.com**

HISTORICAL SKETCHES

OF THE

DISCOVERY, SETTLEMENT,

AND PROGRESS OF EVENTS

IN THE

COOS COUNTRY AND VICINITY,

PRINCIPALLY INCLUDED

Between the Years 1754 and 1785.

By REV. GRANT POWERS, A. M., C. H. S.

HAVERHILL, N. H.
PUBLISHED BY HENRY MERRILL.
1880.

District of Connecticut, ss.

BE IT REMEMBERED, that on the ninth day of March, A. D. 1840, GRANT POWERS, of the said district, hath deposited in this office the title of a book, the title of which is in the words following, to wit :—

"Historical Sketches of the Discovery, Settlement, and Progress of Events in the Coos Country and Vicinity, principally included between the years 1754 and 1785. By Rev. Grant Powers, A. M., C. H. S."

The right whereof he claims as author, in conformity with an act of Congress, entitled "An act to amend the several acts respecting copy rights."

CHARLES A. INGERSOLL,
Clerk of the District of Connecticut.

District of Connecticut, ss.

The foregoing is a true copy of the original record of copy right, recorded March 9th, A. D. 1840.

Attest,   CHARLES A. INGERSOLL,
Clerk of the District.

A true copy of copy right.

GRANT POWERS.

PREFACE.

THE history of our nation is peculiar in a number of things, but in none more than this,—that it records its own origin. There is no other nation that does this, the Jews excepted. No one of the present nations of Europe can tell us a word of their earliest ancestors, or even specify the century in which their territory was first taken possession of by them, but all is involved in obscurity as are the years before the flood. But it is far different with our early history as a nation. We know the men who said they would be free, and who laid the foundation of this mighty republic. We know whence they came, the object for which they came, the *spot* to which they came, and the year, the month, and the day they took possession. Our nation owes a lasting debt of gratitude to our ancestors for their fidelity in recording the incipient steps taken by them in settling this new world. But with regret must we say that their descendants soon began to relax in their fidelity in this respect, and they continued to decline, until their delinquency was almost entire. It may well be doubted, whether more than one-half of the towns in New England have any well-authenticated history of their early settlement, and had not the attention of the people been called to this subject by recently organized Historical Societies, and centennial addresses, a very few years had buried all in oblivion with those towns whose history was not already recorded. There seems, truly, an anomaly in the human character, inasmuch as man delights to retrace the line of his descent to his remotest ancestry, and has a strong passion to live in the memory of his descendants, and yet possesses very little inclination to do anything directly to furnish the means to his posterity of knowing that he ever existed.

One reason for the indifference manifested towards recording present events, is the general impression that they can have no important bearing upon what is to come, unless they are such events as greatly interest the community in present time — the result of a great battle, a revolution in a kingdom, or a destructive earthquake. But nothing is more delusive than such an impression. What would the inhabitants of the city of London now give for the year, the month, and the day, in which the first man pitched his tent on that ground? What would they give if they could know his name, his origin, whence he came, the circumstances in which he came, the object for his coming, and, withal, a minute description of the place as it then was? An octavo pamphlet of ten pages, containing well-authenticated facts of this kind, would be worth millions sterling to the author or proprietor. And the history of our ancestors' landing at Plymouth is infinitely more important in our history than the history of the surrender of Burgoyne's army, or that of Cornwallis. And even those occurrences which do not seem to stand intimately connected with any great results, time will often vest with peculiar interest, in the view of posterity. How unhappy is the reflection, then, that the early settlement of our towns should be permitted to be forever lost through the apathy or indifference of their inhabitants, since the time will certainly arrive when the subject will be duly appreciated, and our descendants will reproach us for our stupidity and sloth in this respect!

It was in view of these and kindred considerations, that the author of the following Sketches commenced, sixteen years ago, visiting the survivors among the first settlers in the Coos country, and in some towns in the vicinity. He was careful to take down their statements in their presence, and they were interrogated upon almost all subjects here introduced. Some made further communications under their own hand-writing, and he has obtained written and published documents, as far as he was able, to aid him in this work. But as it has been his main design to go back of written and published documents, and to bring to light things which would never have appeared, unless they were taken up in a work of this kind, he could avail himself of those documents but in a limited degree; and in general, they are introduced as corroborative testimony, or explanatory, merely. But he fears he has already raised, by his remarks, expectations which he will by no means be able to satisfy; and yet he has done what he could with his means. He could not create means, and yet had procured so many, that he could hardly feel justified in permitting them to perish with himself. It will be perceived that he writes things grave, things trivial, and things important, and this with a view to present as nearly as possible, to the present and future generations, the circumstances, views, feelings, habits and customs of our ancestors.

Before he concludes these remarks, he begs leave to suggest what he views to be important for every family, and for every town in this nation. 1. Let every family obtain as full and as correct a record of their ancestry as is now possible, and every child take a copy, and make additions as time furnishes the means. 2. Let every town have its stated historian, who shall delight in his duty, whose object will be to collect facts of the aged, and by all other means which Providence may afford him; and to record passing events of an interesting nature. Let this record be examined annually by the town authorities and certified by the town clerk, and then preserved in the archives of the town. Extracts from these documents might furnish annually interesting materials in every state for a volume of Historical Collections. And these volumes would in a few years furnish matter for the richest history that ever was possessed by a nation on earth. He suggests it to his brethren in the ministry, of all denominations, to aid in this cause. No class of men in the community enjoy so many facilities for making such a record — none would derive more benefit from it, and it is by no means foreign to their appropriate duties. Brethren, think of it; think seriously, and then act.

GRANT POWERS.

Goshen, Ct., Jan. 1st, 1840.

LIST OF AUTHORITIES

AMONG THE FIRST SETTLERS USED IN THESE SKETCHES.

Col. Joshua Howard.
Hon. James Woodward.
Hon. Ezekiel Ladd.
Mrs. Ruth Ladd.
Mr. Charles Wheeler.
Mrs. Annis Wheeler.
Mr. John Page.
Mrs. Ruth Johnston.
Col. Joshua Bailey.
Mrs. Mary Kent.
Mr. Jonathan Tyler.
Andrew B. Peters, Esq.
John Mann, Esq.
Col. Otis Freeman, Esq.
Rev. Asa Burton, D. D.
Mr. Richard Wallace.
Mr. Joel Strong.
Col. Jonathan Elkins.

OTHER AIDS.

Belknap's History of New Hampshire.
Gazetteer of New Hampshire.
Gazetteer of Vermont.
Eastman's History of Vermont.
Marshall's Life of Washington.
Capt. Powers' Journal.
Rev. Jared Sparks' certified Copies.
David Johnson's Letters and Extracts.
Rev. Clark Perry's Sketches.
John Farmer's Extracts.
Mrs. Abigail Cross.
Mrs. Hannah Pearson.
Mrs. Sally Johnston.

HISTORICAL SKETCHES

OF THE

COOS COUNTRY AND VICINITY.

So late as 1760, there was no settlement by the English, in the Connecticut Valley, above the town of Charlestown, in New Hampshire, which was then called "No. 4." Nor were there more than three towns settled south of Charlestown, in the valley within the present limits of New Hampshire. Hinsdale, or "Fort Dummer," was settled in 1683. Westmoreland, or "No. 2," was settled in 1741; Walpole in 1752.

These towns, with the exception of Walpole, were all settled by Massachusetts men; for, until 1741, it was supposed the north line of Massachusetts would include these towns.

At Hinsdale and Charlestown, forts were built at an early period of their settlement, and soldiers were stationed there for the double purpose of affording protection to the settlers, and arresting the progress

1*

of the Indians from Canada, while meditating incursions upon the frontier towns in Massachusetts.

And so little interest did New Hampshire feel in the settlement of the Connecticut Valley, which has been very justly denominated the "Garden of New England," that in 1745, when the Governor recommended to the Assembly of New Hampshire the taking and sustaining their newly-acquired "Fort Dummer," which fell to them upon the establishment of the line between the two colonies, the lower House declined the acceptance of this place and that of "No. 4;" alleging that the fort was fifty miles distant from any towns settled by New Hampshire; that they did not own the territory; and that they were unequal to the expense of maintaining those places.

Nor was it until 1752, that the Governor of New Hampshire was permitted to adopt any measures to secure to that colony this invaluable tract of country. He then made several grants of townships on both sides of the Connecticut River, and a plan was laid for taking possession of the "Rich Meadows of Cohos,"* of which they had heard by hunters and captives returned.

The original design was to cut a road from "No.

---

* Coos was spelt *Cohos* and *Cowass* by our ancestors.

4" to the Cohos; to lay out two townships, one on each side of the river, and opposite to each other, where Haverhill and Newbury now are. They were to erect stockades, with lodgements for two hundred men, in each township, enclosing a space of fifteen acres; in the centre of which was to be a citadel, containing the public buildings and granaries, which were to be large enough to receive all the inhabitants and their movable effects, in case of necessity. As an inducement for people to remove to this new plantation, they were to have courts of judicature, and other civil privileges, among themselves, and were to be under strict military discipline.

"In pursuance of this plan," says Dr. Belknap, vol. ii. p. 215, "a party was sent up, in the spring of 1752, to view the meadows of Cohos, and lay out the proposed townships." It seems that this project embraced the two objects of possessing the Cohos country, and establishing a military post there. It was to be partly civil and partly military, and a number of adventurers were about to enlist in the enterprise. But the whole plan was defeated by the timely remonstrance of the Indians of the St. Francis tribe. And notwithstanding, Mr. Belknap says, "A party was sent up, in the spring of 1752, to view the meadows of Cohos, and lay out the proposed townships," it is extremely doubtful whether that party ever reached their destination, if they ever left "No. 4." There were no returns made of this tour. They certainly did not lay out the townships. And we find in the Life of General Stark, that in 1754, the General Court of New Hampshire determined to send a party to explore this "*hitherto unknown region,*" referring to the Cohos country.

Now, if this country had been explored by the party of 1752, it could not have been called the "*hitherto* unexplored region" in 1754, seeing that, in each instance, the General Court is represented as the principal mover in these exploring parties. And by the kindness of the late Mr. Farmer, of Concord, N. H., I have been furnished with the extract from Col. Israel Williams' letter, to which Dr. Belknap refers for his authority in saying what he does of the exploring party of 1752. And with the additional evidence which has been obtained upon these transactions since Dr. Belknap's time, I should feel that Col. Williams' letter was insufficient to authorize the assertion, that a party was actually sent into the Cohos country in 1752. It is but a mere allusion to such a thing, or to such an intention.

The letter of Col. Williams was written to the Governor of Massachusetts, dated at Hatfield, 19

March, 1753, and speaks of "our people going to take a view of the *Cowass* meadows last spring." This by no means says they did go to view them, but were "going," or were preparing to go, and view them. And doubtless this was fact. A party might have been sent on by the Governor as far as "No. 4," and even farther; but the Indians remonstrating and threatening, they relinquished their object. Dr. Belknap states that the Indians came to "No. 4," and made this threat; that it was communicated to the Governor of Massachusetts, and he sent the information to the Governor of New Hampshire, and the project was laid aside. The only discrepancy in all this testimony is found in Dr. Belknap's understanding Col. Williams to say that the party of 1752 *did* go into the Cohos country, when he did *not* say it; and as the evidence is now exhibited, we must think he did not mean to say it.

But notwithstanding this project of exploring the Cohos from "No. 4" was suspended, yet the Governor and House of Assembly did by no means abandon the idea of a future possession of those meadows, and events hastened their attempt to explore and possess the Cohos country.

In the spring of 1752, John Stark, afterward *General Stark*, Amos Eastman, afterward of Hollis,

N. H., David Stinson, of Londonderry, and William Stark, were hunting upon Baker's River, in the town of Rumney. They were surprised by a party of ten Indians. John Stark and Amos Eastman were taken prisoners, Stinson was killed, and William Stark escaped by flight. John Stark and Eastman were carried into captivity to the head-quarters of the St. Francis tribe in Canada, and were led directly through the "Meadows," so much talked of in Massachusetts and New Hampshire.

These men returned from their captivity in the summer of 1752, and gave an interesting account of *Cohos;* and as the country was expecting that the war with the French and Indians would soon be renewed, and that the French would be desirous of taking the Cohos country for a military post, the General Court of New Hampshire determined to send a company to explore the region; not to attempt to ascend the Connecticut from "No. 4," but to pursue the track of the Indians as they came from the great valley to Baker's River and the Pemigewasset, and returned again with their prisoners.

Accordingly, in the spring of 1754, Col. Lovewell, Maj. Tolford, and Capt. Page, were sent out at the head of a company, with John Stark for their guide. They left Concord, March 10, 1754, and in seven days made Connecticut River at Piermont. They spent but one night in the valley, and made a precipitate retreat to Concord, at which place they arrived on the thirteenth day from their departure. *

The cause of this failure to explore the region to which they were sent, I have not learned; but that it was a failure, we must know — for one night spent in the woods at Piermont could have returned to the government no information concerning the Coos meadows. The probability was, they feared an Indian foe superior to their own force.

But the government was not discouraged by this failure, and the same season, 1754, Capt. Peter Powers, of Hollis, N. H., Lieut. James Stevens, and Ensign Ephraim Hale, both of Townsend, Mass., were appointed to march at the head of a company to effect, if possible, what had hitherto been attempted in vain. The company rendezvoused at Concord, which was then called Rumford, and commenced their tour on Saturday, June 15, 1754.

It may not be improper to state in this place, that there is no record of this tour in the state papers of that day, and no reference to it in any papers of subsequent date, as I can learn. The evidence of its having been performed consists, at this day, in the

---
* Stark's Life.

tradition among the descendants of Capt. Powers, that he was the first to explore the Coos country, and in his manuscript journal, kept by himself during his tour, recently found among papers on file, preserved by the late Samson Powers, of Hollis, youngest son of the said Peter Powers. I have also the same *tin safe*, of ample dimensions, which contained his journal, and a piece of his *tent cloth* which was spread over him at night, on this very expedition.

The only rational explanation that can be given for the silence of all public records in relation to this exploring tour, may be found in the loose manner in which such things were transacted at that day, and in the commotion which immediately followed Capt. Powers' return; for already war was renewed in Europe between France and England, and the intelligence of it having reached Quebec, the Indians renewed their incursions upon our frontier towns, and made a descent upon Boscawen a few days after the return of the exploring company. This suspended all further thought of settling the Coos country during the war that was then raging, and Capt. Powers' report was not called for, or it was lost during that war, or the war of the Revolution, which followed hard upon the restoration of peace between France and England.

Capt. Powers' journal is not entire—some pages of the returning expedition are lost, and, probably, some prefatory remarks. I should think, also, that it is not as full in description as he would have returned to government, but general facts noted to enable him to make out a correct statement in things essential; and, finally, it is an interesting document of antiquity, and must be so, especially, to the people of Coos, who have for a long time felt an earnest desire to know who first explored that part of the *Great Valley.* I shall give the journal as it is found, only correcting some of the orthography, and offering some explanation in notes.

JOURNAL.

"*Saturday, June* 15th, 1754. This day left Rumford," (now Concord,) "and marched to Contoocook, which is about eight miles, and here tarried all night."

[The original Indian name of Concord was Penacook. From 1733 it bore the name of Rumford, until 1762, and then took the name Concord.]

"*Sunday, June* 16th. This day tarried at Contoocook, and went to meeting, and tarried here all this night."

[Contoocook was present Boscawen. The Rev.

Phinehas Stevens was minister in this place at that time.]

Monday, June 17th. This morning fair weather, and we fixed our packs, and went and put them on board our canoes, about nine of the clock, and some of the men went in the canoes, and the rest on the shore. And so we marched up the River Merrimack to the crotch, or parting thereof; and then up the Pemigewasset about one mile and a half, and camped above the carrying-place, which carrying-place is about one hundred rods long; and the whole of this day's march is thirteen miles.

Tuesday, June 18th. This day marched up the Pemigewasset River, about eight miles, to Smith's River, and then east one hundred rods, and then north, two hundred and twenty rods, to the long carrying-place on Pemigewasset River, and there camped."

[This encampment, I think, must have been on or near the present line which divides Bristol from New Chester upon the Pemigewasset. It might be interesting to the present inhabitants of those towns to mark out the spot which was thus occupied by swords and bristling bayonets in 1754, whilst the whole country around remained an unbroken wilderness. And what may be true in this case, may be true of others in respect to all places hereafter to be named by the exploring party.]

"*Wednesday, June* 19th. We marched on our journey, and carried across the long carrying-place on Pemigewasset River two miles northeast, which land hath a good soil, beech and maple, with a good quantity of large masts. From the place where we put in the canoes, we steered east, north-east, up the river about one mile, and then we steered north-east one mile, and north six miles up to Sawheganet Falls, where we carried by about four rods; and from the falls we steered about north-east, to Pemigewasset interval, two miles, and from the beginning of the interval we made good our course north four miles, and there camped on a narrow point of land. The last four miles the river was extremely crooked."

"*Thursday, June* 20th. We steered our course, one turn with another, which were great turns, west, north-west, about two miles and a half, to the crotch, or parting of the Pemigewasset River, at Baker's River mouth; thence from the mouth of Baker's River, up said river, north-west by west, six miles. This river is extraordinary crooked, and good interval. Thence up the river about two miles north-west, and there we shot a moose, the sun about a half an hour high, and there camped."

[This must have been in the town of Rumney.]

"*Friday, June* 21st. We steered up the said Baker's River with our canoes about five miles as the river ran, which was extraordinary crooked. In the after part of this day, there was a great shower of '*haile and raine,*' which prevented our proceeding any further, and here we camped; and here left our canoes, for the water in the river was so shoal that we could not go with them any further."

"*Saturday, June* 22d. This morning was dark and cloudy weather; but after ten of the clock, it cleared off hot, and we marched up the river near the Indian carrying-place, from Baker's River to Connecticut River, and there camped, and could not go any further by reason of a great shower of rain, which held almost all this afternoon."

"*Sunday, June* 23d. This morning dark and cloudy weather, and we marched up this river about one mile, and came to the Indian carrying-place, and, by reason of the dark weather, we were obliged to follow the marked way, that way marked by Major Lovewell and Capt. Tolford, and others, from Baker's River to Connecticut River. And this day's march was but about six miles; and we camped between the two first Baker Ponds. And it came on a great storm of rain, which prevented our marching any further. And on this day's march we saw a consid-

erable quantity of white pine timber, and found it
was something large, fit for thirty-inch masts, as we
judged. But before this day's march, we saw no
white pine timber, that was very large, on this Baker's
River, but a great quantity of small white pine, fit
for boards and small masts. And on this river there
is a great quantity of excellent interval, from the beginning of it to the place where we left this river.
And it layeth of a pretty equal proportion from one
end to the other; and back of the interval, there is
a considerable quantity of large mountains."

[Those more familiarly acquainted with the serpentine course of Baker's River than the writer, may fix
on several encampments in Rumney and Wentworth
with tolerable accuracy; but we shall all agree that,
at this last date, they were encamped between the
Baker Ponds, lying in the north-east part of the present town of Orford. It is a little singular that it
should not have been discovered until recently, that
the south-western branch of Baker's River afforded
greater facilities for communication between the Connecticut Valley and Pemigewasset than those routes
which have been hitherto improved, seeing the Indians had given their preference to this south branch,
and it was improved by the first English parties
which explored the country.]

"*Monday, June* 24th. This morning it rained hard, and all the night past, and it held raining all this day, and we kept our camp, and here we stayed the night ensuing, and it rained almost all night."

"*Tuesday, June* 25th. This morning fair weather, and we swung our packs, the sun about a half an hour high, and we marched along the carrying-place, or road marked, about two miles, and then steered our course north, twelve degrees west, about twelve miles, and came to that part of the Coos interval that is called *Moose Meadow*. And then steered our course up the river by the side of the interval, about northeast, and came to a large stream that came into the interval, which is here about a mile wide. This stream came out of the east, and we camped here this night. There are on this river the best falls and conveniences for all sorts of mills. These falls are nearly twenty feet perpendicular."

["*Moose Meadow*" must have been the Indian name for that part of Coos which they made first, and I am quite confident that some of the old people whom I consulted relative to the first settlements, called the meadow owned by Major Merrill, in Piermont, "Moose Meadow;" but I have no minute of it, and as at that time I had no knowledge of this document, I was not particular to retain the locality of *Moose Meadow*.

But we at length find the company encamped upon the banks of the Oliverian in Haverhill, which river was then without a name, as well as Haverhill itself. They passed along, he says, "by the side of the interval,"—that is, at the foot of the hill where the meadows commence. He says the interval was "*here about a mile wide.*" He meant on both sides of the river. He calls the Oliverian a "large stream." The heavy rains, he has already described, rendered it such. The falls, I should think, were accurately described. He does not tell us on which side of the Oliverian he made his encampment; probably south, upon the elevated platform formerly owned by Richard Gookin; or, if he crossed the river that night, he would select the dry spot where stands the dwelling-house of the late Capt. Joseph Pearson. Permit me, kind reader, to add a reflection. How dark is the future with all to whom God has not revealed what his future Providences shall be ! Capt. Powers, when he camped upon the banks of the Oliverian, must have marched in his meandering course at least seventy miles, without seeing a human habitation ! And what had been his astonishment, if it had been revealed to him that night, that his first-born son should be the minister of a church and people in that place, in a less time than eleven years ; that he should sustain that relation nearly twenty years; and that his grandson, by his own youngest son, should hold the same station about fifteen years, from the fifty-seventh to the seventy-second year after his decease! This would have been an astounding vision, but no more than what time has fulfilled.]

"*Wednesday, June* 26th. This morning fair weather, and we marched up the interval to the great turn of clear interval, which is the uppermost part of the clear interval, on the westerly side of Connecticut River, and there came a great shower of rain, which held almost all this afternoon; and we camped by the river on the easterly side, above all the clear interval; and this day's march was about six miles, and very crooked."

[It will appear, as we advance in these sketches, that the Little Ox Bow on Haverhill side, and the Great Ox Bow on Newbury side, were cleared interval when the first settlers came in. They had been cleared and cultivated to some extent by the Indians, and this is the fact to which the journal alludes. Their encampment was on the well-known Porter place.]

"*Thursday, June* 27th. This morning it was cloudy weather, and it began to rain, the sun about an hour high, and we marched, nothwithstanding, up the river to Amonoosuck River, and our course was about north, distance about five miles ; and we camped here, for the River Amonoosuck was so high we could not go over it without a canoe ; for it was swift water, and near twenty rods wide. This afternoon it cleared off fair, and we went about our canoe, and partly built it. Some of our men went up the River Amonoosuck, to see what discoveries they could make ; and they discovered excellent land, and a considerable quantity of large white pines."

"*Friday, June* 28th. This morning fair weather, and we went about the canoe, and completed the same by about twelve of the clock this day, and went over the river ; and we concluded to let the men go down the river in the canoe, who were not likely to perform the remaining part of the journey, by reason of sprains in the ankles, and weakness of body. They were four in number ; and we steered our course for the great interval about east, north-east ; and we this day marched, after we left the river, about ten miles. And the land was exceedingly good upland, and some quantity of white pine, but not thick, but some of them fit for masts."

[These four men, it would seem, were about to take their chance upon the river, and to return by the way of Charlestown.]

"*Saturday, June* 29th. This morning was cloudy but we swung our packs, and steered our course about north-east, ten miles, and came to Connecticut River. There it came on rainy, and we camped by the side of the river, and it rained all this afternoon, and we kept our camp all this night. The land was, this day's march, very good, and it may be said as good as ever was seen by any of us. The common growth of wood was beech and maple, and not thick at all. It hath a great quantity of small brooks. This day and the day past, there were about three brooks fit for corn-mills; and these were the largest of the brooks that we saw."

[It seems that the march of the two last days was made between the valley of the Connecticut, and that of the Amonoosuck, upon the high lands of Bath, Lyman, and Littleton, and we now find them encamped in the southern part of Dalton.]

"*Sunday, June* 30th. This morning exceeding rainy weather, and it rained all the night past, and continued raining until twelve of the clock this day; and after that, it was fair weather, and we marched along up Connecticut River; and our course we made good this day, was about five miles, east by north, and there came to a large stream, which came from the south-east. This river is about three rods wide, and we called it *Stark's* River, by reason of Ensign John Stark's being found by the Indians at the mouth of this river. This river comes into the Connecticut at the foot of the upper interval, and thence we travelled up the interval about seven miles, and came to a large river which came from the southeast; and it is about five rods wide. Here we concluded to go no further with the full scout, by reason of our provisions being almost all spent; and almost all our men had worn out their shoes. This river we called *Powers'* River, it being the camping place at the end of our journey; and there we camped by the river."

[It seems that John Stark had been taken twice by the Indians while on his hunting expeditions—once on Stark's River, and once on Baker's River. The river which they named Stark's River runs through Dalton, and is now called John's River, because Stark's name was John, perhaps; but I think they had better preserved the original name, and this would have perpetuated a historical fact, and borne up a name that the whole town would delight to cherish among them; but who is to know whether this is John Stark's River, or John Smith's River, or any other John's River? The river they called *Powers'* River is in Lancaster, and is now called

Israel's River. This, too, I think, ought to bear the name they gave it, instead of a wandering, and perhaps a worthless hunter. Capt. Powers was the first man of English descent who ever visited that town for discovery. He did it in imminent peril, and for the good of his country. How much more gratifying it would be to the present inhabitants of that town, and to all future generations of theirs, did they bear upon their river the name of the first man who ever by authority discovered their town! There has been much wrong in these things in many of our towns. Our worthy ancestors, who bore the toils and went through the perils of exploring and settling our forests, and of subduing them, richly merited this cheap method of perpetuating a memorial of themselves. I do not attach blame to the people of Lancaster for this—for they may not know, to this day, that such a company ever visited their town, or that their river was ever formally named by persons under authority; but these are the facts. There is no record in the journal of any transaction on the first day of July. It was probably spent in inactivity and rest.]

"*Tuesday, July* 2d. This morning fair weather, and we thought proper to mend our shoes, and to return homeward; and accordingly we went about the same; and whilst the men were this way engaged, the captain, with two of his men, marched up the river to see what further discoveries they could make, and they travelled about five miles, and there they discovered where the Indians had a large camping place, and had been making canoes, and had not been gone above one or two days at most; and so they returned to the rest of the men again about twelve of the clock; and then we returned, and marched down the river to Stark's River, and there camped. This afternoon it rained hard, but we were forced to travel for want of provisions. This interval is exceedingly large, and the farther up the larger. The general course of this river is from north-east by east, as far as the interval extends."

[The captain and his two men penetrated, probably, as far as present Northumberland, and must have travelled nearly one hundred and forty miles after they left the habitations of civilized men. At Northumberland they first fell upon the trail of Indians, where they had, probably, been preparing themselves canoes to enable them to descend upon our frontier settlements.]

"*Wednesday, July* 3d. This morning cloudy, weather, and thundered; and after the sun an hour high, it rained hard, and continued about an hour, and then we swung packs, and steered our course west-south-west, aiming for Amonoosuck River ; and this day we marched about fourteen miles, and camped."

[We shall perceive that, for the last twelve days of their march, the rain had fallen in unusual abundance for that season of the year ; and it would not be strange if they spoke of some small streams as larger than they are ordinarily found, especially since the clearing of the country ; but as far as my knowledge extends, they were not far from present truth concerning them ; and as it regards distances, they were remarkably accurate, seeing they were in a wilderness, followed the course of streams, and did not carry a chain.]

"*Thursday, July* 4th. We marched on our course west-south-west, and this day we marched about twenty miles, and camped."

[This was the day on which the Delegates from six of the Colonies signed, at Albany, articles of union for mutual government and defence, anticipating the renewal of war between France and England, "exactly twenty-two years before the declaration of American independence."—*Belknap.*]

"*Friday, July* 5th. We marched about three miles to our packs at Amonoosuck, the same course we had steered heretofore; and we afterwards went over Connecticut River, and looked up Wells' River, and camped a little below Wells' River this night."

[At the west end of the bridge, perhaps, leading from Haverhill to Wells' River.]

"*Saturday, July* 6th. Marched down the great river to Great Coos, and crossed the river below the great turn of clear interval, and there left the great river, and steered south by east about three miles, and there camped. Here was the best of upland, and some quantity of large white pines."

[I think they crossed into Haverhill at the "Dow Farm," so called, and the three miles brought them to Haverhill Corner, and their description of it answers to the description given by the first settlers. I would say to the people of Haverhill Corner, that eighty-five years ago, on the sixth of July last, (1839,) your Common was the encampment of an exploring company, sent out by the government of England; that this company felt themselves surrounded by a vast wilderness; and, while the towering trees of the forest formed their canopy, they confided in their own vigilance and prowess, under God, to protect them from beasts of prey and savage men. Well may you exclaim, while in your ceiled houses, and while surveying from your windows your ample fields and meadows, *What hath God wrought?*]

I must inform the reader that, at this point of time, the journal ceases to speak of their homeward march, and no trace of the remainder can be found. We are left to suppose that they retraced their steps the way they came, with hostile Indians pressing hard in their rear; for we learn from Belknap that by the fifteenth of August, of that year, they were at Bakerstown and vicinity, (now Salisbury,) killing and taking captive the inhabitants.

From this time until the fall of Quebec into the possession of the British in 1759, no more efforts were made to discover and settle new territories, but every man had as much as he could do to retain what he had already in possession. Nor does it appear that any steps were taken towards the settlement of the Connecticut Valley in 1760; for our men were still employed in Canada in gathering up the fragments of the French armies which were stationed in different places, and had not as yet surrendered to the English. But in 1761, when the Colonies no longer feared the incursions of the French and Indians upon their frontier towns, the spirit of emigration from the older settlements, and of extending their possessions, revived, and surpassed all that had been before witnessed. Men from Connecticut, Massachusetts, and New Hampshire were now preparing to

OF THE COOS COUNTRY. 33

transplant themselves into the then great western valley of the Connecticut, and the Governor of New Hampshire did not let slip the golden opportunity of filling his coffers. In every township granted to petitioners, five hundred acres of land were reserved for the Governor, without fees or charges, and he was well rewarded by petitioners for his services. No less than sixty townships were granted on the west side of Connecticut River, and eighteen on the east side, in the year 1761. At this time, New Hampshire claimed all the land west to New York line.

The reason which Mr. Belknap gives for the great rush into the Connecticut Valley at this time is, that the continual passing of troops through these lands during the war, caused the value of them to be more generally known. This was undoubtedly true, especially after the successes of the English at Ticonderoga, Crown Point, and in Canada in 1759. There was then no danger to be apprehended from the enemy, and it is not reasonable to suppose that Massachusetts and New Hampshire men, returning from those successful campaigns, would make the tour of Lake Champlain and North River to Albany, rather than cross the highlands of Vermont, and descend the Connecticut River, a tour which some of them must have previously made while captives to the French and Indians. *2

This fact, in connection with Capt. Powers' journal of an earlier date by some years, convinces me that the traditionary tales which have been so long rife in the Coos country, that their fathers were indebted for the discovery of their country to Major Rogers' famished men, as they fled from the infuriated Indians of the St. Francis tribe in 1759, are all apocryphal. The truth is, when Major Rogers disbanded his men for their greater safety, he appointed them to rendezvous at the *Upper Coos*, says Belknap; which could not have been done, if the place had not been known. Some of Rogers' men, no doubt, made the Coos, and some passed through it, whilst others there perished, whose remains were found by the first settlers; but those who survived that disastrous retreat were the last men in the world to give a description of the country through which they passed, whilst hunger, like an armed man, was threatening them with dissolution at every step.

The tradition, that speaks of a company of men sent up the river as far as Coos, for the relief of Rogers' men, and of their returning just when Rogers' men came up to witness the yet living embers of the fires they had left behind them, must also be fabulous. Rogers left Crown Point with two hundred rangers on the thirteenth of September, 1759, to destroy the Indians at St. Francis, who had committed so many depredations and cruelties upon our border inhabitants. They were sent out with the utmost secrecy. On the 5th of October he struck the fatal blow, and commenced his retreat, which terminated disastrously to many. How could the people of New Hampshire know of this expedition? How in *time* to make this provision? And how could they know that their aid would be needed, or *where* it would be needed?

The probability is, that the Indians discovered the exploring party of Captain Powers in 1754, and related the fact to the early settlers, and imagination soon connected the two events of Powers' exploration and Rogers' retreat, giving the latter as the cause of the former. My view of this subject is, that the first information which our people received of the "Coos Meadows" was derived from Indians, hunters, and captives. The second source of intelligence was from Captain Powers and his company. And the third was from the soldiers of the old French war. But it is time that I proceed to the settlement of the "*Cohos Meadows.*"

There were two men who were the principal agents in the first settlement of Haverhill and Newbury in the Coos country, Col. Jacob Bailey, of Newbury,

Mass., and Capt. John Hazen, of Haverhill, Mass. They were both officers in the old French war, and stood high in the estimation of government. It is supposed that they were taught to expect each a charter of a township in the Coos, if they went on and commenced settlements therein. They agreed to act in conjunction, and to proceed harmoniously in the undertaking. Hazen was to go on first, and take possession of the east side of the river, and Bailey was to take possession of the west side as soon as he could find persons to do it, and come on himself as soon as his affairs at home would permit.

Accordingly, Capt. Hazen sent on two men with his cattle in the summer of 1761, viz., Michael Johnston and John Pettie. They came from Haverhill, Mass., by No. 4, or Charlestown, and then up the Connecticut River. They took possession of the *Little Ox Bow*, on the east side of the river, in the north parish of Haverhill, N. H. They found this Ox Bow, and the Great Ox Bow on the west side of the river, "*cleared interval*," according to what Capt. Powers states in his journal; and they had in former years been cultivated by the Indians for the growth of Indian corn. The hills were swarded over, and a tall wild grass grew spontaneously and luxuriantly, so that an abundance of fodder for the cattle was easily procured.

The Indians dwelt at this time on these meadows, east and west of the river, and were amicable. The loss of their strong ally, the French, and the chastisement which Rogers inflicted upon their brethren at St. Francis, had cooled their ardor, and rendered the idea of our men taking possession of those meadows far more acceptable to them than it was in 1752, when they threatened war in case the country was explored for the purpose of settlement. It was not wonderful that the Indians should feel deep repugnance at the idea of losing this country. It was a fine country for them. It was easy of cultivation, and suited to their imperfect means. The soil was rich. The river abounded in salmon, and the streams in trout, and the whole country was plentifully supplied with game, bear, deer, moose, and fowls. It was the half-way resting place between the Canadas and the shores of the Atlantic; and while this was retained, it was the key that opened the door to, or shut it against, the most direct communication between the Colonies and the Canadas. And, what was more than all to the Indians, it was their fathers' sepulchre.

I cannot but marvel somewhat at the conclusion of the Rev. Clark Perry, in his "Annals and Historical Sketches of Newbury, Vt., 1831." He says, p. 24,

"It does not appear that this section of country was ever the permanent abode of Indians." But why it should not have been, I cannot conjecture. Certainly there was no spot in New England which could have presented to the Indian greater inducements for a permanent abode; and we know of no one place in New England which has exhibited stronger indications of Indian settlements.

I have a communication from David Johnson, Esq., of Newbury, touching this point, and I think the evidence he gives of an old Indian settlement in that place is conclusive. No man is better qualified to judge impartially and correctly in this matter than Mr. Johnson. He has always lived on the place of which he speaks, and he is a gentleman who feels the liveliest interest in antiquities; has been accumulating facts of this kind for many years; and I would embrace this opportunity to express my obligations to him for his prompt and persevering aid in the work before me. I shall put down his communication as I have received it.

"On the high ground, east of the mouth of Cow Meadow Brook, and south of the three large projecting rocks, were found many indications of an old and extensive Indian settlement. There were many domestic implements. Among the rest were a stone mortar and pestle. The pestle I have seen. Heads of arrows, large quantities of ashes, and the ground burnt over to a great extent, are some of the marks of a long residence there. The burnt ground and ashes were still visible the last time it was ploughed. On the meadow, forty or fifty rods below, near the rocks in the river, was evidently a burying ground. The remains of many of the sons of the forest are there deposited. Bones have frequently been turned up by the plough. That they were buried in the sitting posture, peculiar to the Indians, has been ascertained."

"When the first settlers came here, the remains of a fort were still visible on the Ox Bow, a dozen or twenty rods from the east end of Moses Johnson's lower garden, on the south side of the lane. The size of the fort was plain to be seen. Trees about as large as a man's thigh were growing in the circumference of the old fort. A profusion of white flint-stones and heads of arrows may yet be seen scattered over the ground. It is a tradition which I have frequently heard repeated, that after the fight with Lovewell, the Indians said they should now be obliged to leave Coossuck." *

It will appear in the sequel of these sketches, that

---

* Our Coos.

at a remote period, there was an intimate connection between the Indians of Coos, of Maine, and of the St. Francis. The connection between the Coos and St. Francis tribe continued until the last.

We now return to Johnston and Pettie, whom we have left on the Little Ox Bow. They made themselves a booth, and built a shed for their cattle, and spent the subsequent winter in feeding out the hay they had gathered during the summer. One would suppose that these individuals must have felt themselves sufficiently solitary from November, 1761, to June, 1762, not having, for a great part of this time, a white man within sixty miles of them, yet surrounded with Indians, and their cattle a temptation for the latter to massacre them, that they might seize upon the booty. But they survived the winter unharmed, and in the spring of 1762, Capt. Hazen came to their relief, with hands and materials for building a grist-mill and saw-mill, where the Swazey mills now stand.

But before Capt. Hazen arrived, a family had come into Newbury, by the name of Sleeper. In March, 1762, Glazier Wheeler, from Shutesbury, Mass., came up with a brother of his, to hunt near the head of the Connecticut River, and while on the way, they fell in with Samuel Sleeper and his family, at Charlestown. They were from Hampton, N. H. Sleeper was a Quaker preacher, but was now employed by General Jacob Bailey to proceed to Newbury, and take possession until the general could come on in person. Sleeper contracted with Wheeler to take him and his family on to his semi-sleigh and semi-sled, and carry them to Newbury.

Sleeper pitched his tent a little south of where the Kents now live, and have long lived. Thomas Chamberlain next came from Dunstable, N. H., and settled on "Mushquash Meadow," south of the "Great Ox Bow," and a little at the north-west of the ferry at the Dow farm. Richard Chamberlain came on next from Hinsdale, N. H., and settled on Mushquash Meadow. Chamberlain landed at the ferry about noon with his family. Before night, a hut was erected of posts and bark, which served them three months for a habitation. In the centre stood a large stump, which was their table. The house he afterward erected stood near Josiah Little's barn, not far from the river. The old cellar may yet be seen.

These two Chamberlains were not in the interest of Hazen or Bailey, but were employed to come on and take possession for one Oliver Willard, of Northfield, Mass., who was endeavoring to supplant Bailey and Hazen. But the latter being united in their petitions for grants; being also in favor with the Governor, and having taken possession by their agents prior to Willard, succeeded, and Willard failed. Willard's disappointment was great, and his anger violent. He gave out vaunting threats that if he could catch Hazen out of the settlement, he would flog him to his heart's content. Hazen, however, had seen too many tomahawks and bristling bayonets around the walls of Quebec to be greatly disquieted by a threat of this kind. But these two men afterward met in Charlestown, and upon Willard's attempting to execute his promise, he caught the severest flogging that any man need receive, and this terminated the matter.

This same year, 1762, John Hazleton, from Hampstead, N. H., moved into Newbury, and first lived at the foot of the hill, south of the Johnson village, but afterward settled in the south part of the town, where Col. Moody Chamberlain now lives, near the south bridge. In this family, in 1763, before they moved from the Ox Bow, the first English child was born in this town—Betsey Hazleton, now the Widow Lovewell, of the north parish in Haverhill, in her 77th year.

The same year, the first male child of English descent was born in the family of Thomas Chamberlain, and was called Jacob Bailey Chamberlain. The parents of this son received a hundred acres of land, as a bounty, according to a promise of the original proprietor, that the first mother of a son born in that settlement should receive one hundred acres of land.

I now return to Hazen and his party. I have said he came on in the spring of 1762, with men and materials for building a saw-mill and grist-mill where the Swazey mills now stand. With Hazen came Col. Joshua Howard, of Haverhill, Mass., born April 24, 1740. He was then 22 years of age, and lived in Haverhill until January 7th, 1839, almost 99 years of age. He was a man of strict veracity, and at the time when he gave his narration of events in the early settlement of these towns (July 27, 1824), he was of sound mind and good memory. I am much indebted to him for materials in these sketches.

Howard labored that first season in preparing the timbers for the mills, and was present at the raising of them. He relates one providential escape from death at the raising of those mills, which deserves notice. One of their company, John Hughs, an Irishman, fell from the frame, sixteen feet, and struck perpendicularly upon the mud-sill, head downwards, without any thing to abate the force of the fall. He was taken up without signs of life; but Glazier Wheeler, from Newbury, found a penknife with the company, and opened a vein, and after the loss of blood, he revived, and soon recovered from the tremendous blow. Physicians and surgeons, those comfortable adjuncts to an improved state of society, were then out of the question, and every mind, in such an emergency, was put upon its own resources. But I have a tale more melancholy to relate.

Johnson and Pettie, who had spent the winter in solitariness, now thought of visiting their friends at the east; and preparing themselves a canoe, they took their departure in June, intending to descend the river to Charlestown. They made their way pleasantly until they came near the mouth of White River, in Lebanon. Here they were drawn into a whirlpool; their canoe was upset, and they were plunged into the river. Johnston made every effort to reach the shore, but sunk into the arms of death. Pettie, being the better swimmer, gained the shore, and was enabled to bear the melancholy tidings of Johnston's death to his friends.

Some time after this event, a stranger, passing up the river in a boat, discovered the body of a man lying upon the shore of a small island in the river between Lebanon, N. H., and Hartford, Vt. Not knowing anything of Johnston or of his fate, and being far from any settlement, he performed the kindest office to a stranger corpse which remained in his power. He digged a grave in the best manner he could, interred the body, and left it the sole proprietor of the island. It now bears his name, "Johnston's Island." He is still the only occupant, and will probably remain such, until the Great Proprietor of the world shall assert his claim, recall the dead, and extinguish all earthly titles. Col. Charles Johnston, brother of Michael Johnston, after he came to Haverhill, and learned the resting place of his brother, went down to the island, found the lonely grave, bedewed it with his tears, erected a monument to his brother's memory, and resigned all into the keeping of him who had given and taken. Capt. Michael Johnston, now of Haverhill, was so called to bear up and perpetuate the name of that uncle who found this early grave.

Col. Howard relates that he and two others were the first among the settlers who came from Salisbury in a straight course to Haverhill. They came on in April, 1762. Howard, Jesse Harriman, and Simeon Stevens employed an old hunter at Concord to guide them through. They came west of Newfound Pond, in Hebron, followed up the north-west branch of Baker's River into Coventry, and down the Oliverian to the Connecticut. They performed the journey in four days from Concord.

In June, of this year, the first family moved into Haverhill. Uriah Morse, and Hannah, his wife, came from Northfield, Mass., and settled upon the bank of Poole Brook, west of the bridge on the main road, and a little south-west of the house where David Merrill lived for many years. They boarded Capt. Hazen's men, while they were building the mills, and other adventurers as they came into the settlement. The first child of English descent had its birth in this family, in the spring of 1763; but we hear of no bounty bestowed upon the parents, as in Newbury, the same year, nor do we learn whether it was male or female. Indeed, it survived its birth but a few days. The first death of an adult occurred in this family, also — Polly Harriman died of consumption, aged 18 years. She was buried a little south-west of the present meeting-house in the north parish of Haverhill, between the meeting-house and the Southards. Her death was much lamented.

Poole Brook derived its name from a man whose name was Poole, who lived fifty or sixty rods north of Uriah Morse's house. Poole was drowned one mile above the *Narrows,* in Connecticut River, above Wells' River. Glazier Wheeler and his son Charles found the body of Poole, seven days after drowning, and it was brought down to the great Ox Bow and interred. Polly, the only child of Mr. Poole, married John Johnson, of Newbury, and was drowned in the Connecticut, near where her father was buried.

Thomas Johnson, Timothy Bedel, Capt. Hazen, and Jesse Harriman boarded in the family of Uriah Morse in the autumn of 1762. Johnson was now in his 21st year. He was born March 22, 1742, and came into the settlement in the service of General Bailey; but the first season he boarded on the east side of the river. He originated in Haverhill, Mass. Thomas Johnson's first purchase in Newbury bears date October 6, 1763. It is the united testimony of the first settlers, that at that early period, moose, bear, deer, beaver, otter, mink and sables were numerous, and that salmon enriched and adorned the river. Trout was not so abundant in the streams as salmon in the river, and shad never appeared above Bellows' Falls, in Walpole.

We now come to speak of the events of 1763, in those settlements. This was the year of charters with them. Newbury's charter bears date March 18, 1763, signed by Benning Wentworth, and I think Haverhill charter bears the same date.

The first town meeting under the charter was held by the freemen of Newbury, June 13, 1763, and not less than 100 miles from the location of their grant, viz., at Plaistow, N. H. And before this meeting was adjourned, they voted to unite with Haverhill in paying a preacher for the term of two or three months, "this fall or winter,"— a very worthy example, while they were yet so few and feeble.

This was a year of enlargement with Haverhill and Newbury. Benjamin Hall, from Massachusetts, came in and settled near the Porter place, where the Southards now live. Jonathan Saunders and Sarah Rowell, both from Hampton, N. H., came and settled near the present house of Dr. Carleton, late deceased. Jacob Hall, from Northfield, Mass., came and settled on the Dow farm, so called. Hon. James Woodward, of Hampstead, N. H., came and settled on his place at the age of twenty-two years. He purchased his farm at twenty cents per acre. Mr. John Page, father of the present governor of New Hampshire, came into Haverhill this year from Lunenburg, Mass. He was employed by his uncle, David Page, to assist in driving up his cattle to Lancaster, and this was the beginning of the settlement of that town — David Page's son having been up in the preceding June of that year, and marked out a way for them from Haverhill. John Page returned from Lancaster, and bought his farm in Haverhill, but spent the subsequent winter in taking care of Gen. Bailey's stock in Newbury, which arrived that season, and not in 1762, as many have supposed. This was Mr. Page's account, Captain Howard's, and Col. Joshua Bailey's, who came with his father to Newbury in 1764, at eleven years of age. Page continued to labor for Gen. Bailey until he was able to pay for his farm. He then came to Haverhill, married Abigail Saunders, daughter of the first settler south of him, and lived to the age of eighty-two, and departed this life in 1823.

This year Noah White came into Newbury, with his family, and settled. Thomas Johnson established himself in the Ox Bow, and Col. Jacob Kent came into Newbury, November 4, 1763, the twelfth family in both towns. There were a number of young men boarding in those families. Col. Kent was born at Chebacco, Mass., June 11, 1726, and Mary White, his wife, was born at Plaistow, N. H., August 14, 1736. Mrs. Kent survived her husband many years, and lived to a great age. She was nearly ninety years of age when I visited her to obtain information relative to the first settlers, and I found her memory good upon subjects of ancient date. In answer to the question, "Were there many wild animals in the town when you first came here, such as bears and wolves?" she replied, "O, yes, there were enough of them creatures! I was once frightened almost out of my wits by them. It was on a Sabbath day. The colonel was gone to meeting, and I was left alone, and there came three great bears to the door, and looked right in upon me! I expected nothing but they would come in and devour me; but after looking at me awhile, they turned away, and trotted off, and glad was I." Ladies of Newbury and Haverhill, how would *you* like, at this time, to have your devotions interrupted, or your domestic concerns thus unceremoniously inspected, by stranger gentlemen, such as these? Mum!

In this year, says Col. Joshua Bailey, John Foreman and several others of Pennsylvania, having enlisted into the British army near the commencement of the old French war, and having been retained in Canada after peace was restored, deserted and made through the woods until they came upon the head waters of the Connecticut, and following down the stream, they came into the north part of Haverhill. But here they found themselves famishing through lack of sustenance, and as they knew not that there was an English settlement within a hundred miles of them, they were prepared to seize upon any thing which could satisfy the demands of hunger. They unexpectedly came in sight of a horse upon the plain north of the north parish meeting-house, and supposing it to be wild, or one that had gone far astray, they shot it, and fed themselves upon its flesh. Replenishing their packs with the residue of the meat, they proceeded south, but soon discovered smokes ascending from chimneys on the Ox Bow and vicinity. They were alarmed at the idea of falling into the hands of hostile Indians, especially since they had killed one of their horses. But after some consultation, they concluded that one of their number should cross the river, make what discoveries he could, and then return and report. He accordingly swam the river, and, to his great joy, found these were English settlements. The news and a boat were soon carried back to his companions. They were brought on to the Ox Bow, where they found food, a shelter, and sympathizing friends. Col. Bailey says, this fact of their killing the horse on that plain gave the name " Horse Meadow" to that section of the town, and not the traditionary story of horses finding a *rush grass* there sooner in the spring than elsewhere.

At this time, 1763, we are told, there were no roads in any direction, and that their bread-stuffs were brought from Charlestown in boats. It is a little extraordinary that none of the first settlers make mention of the great drought which prevailed in the Colonies for the years 1761 and 1762.* It must have affected them whatever were their seasons at Coos; for as yet they were depending on foreign supplies.

We now come to speak of the progress of these settlements in 1764. This was a year of increase, and they realized an accession which seemed to give character to the settlements for many years. Deacon Jonathan Elkins with his family, from Hampton, N. H., came into Haverhill, and settled near Doctor Carleton's. Deacon Elkins was a valuable acquisition to the town; but he remained here but little more than ten years, before he removed to Peacham, Vt., and was one of the first settlers, and most efficient, in that town. Col. Timothy Beedel, from New-Salem, moved his family to this place, and settled on Poole Brook, where David Merrill long lived. Hon. Ezekiel Ladd came in and settled on the place where he lived fifty-four years, and died at the advanced age of eighty years, (1818.) He married Ruth Hutchins. They both belonged to Haverhill, Mass. Mrs. Ladd died 1817, aged seventy-six.

Newbury was enlarged and blessed, also, this year,

---

* See Belknap, vol. ii. p. 238.

by the arrival of Gen. Jacob Bailey with his family. He had been from the first the principal mover in the settlement. His influence was felt in every proceeding, and now he had come to bless himself, and to save much people alive, in the approaching contest between Great Britain and her Colonies. He arrived in Newbury, October, 1764. He lived, at that time, south of the Johnson Village, and north of the hill, on the east side of the road. He was thirty-eight years of age when he came to Newbury, and lived until March, 1815, when he resigned a long life, that had been devoted to his country, to his town, and, for a considerable length of time, to his God. He died at eighty-nine years of age.

This same year came the Rev. Peter Powers, of Hollis, N. H., to labor with this people in holy things. Mr. Powers was born in Dunstable, N. H., November 29, 1728, moved to Hollis with his father, January, 1731, which was the first settlement in that town. He graduated at Harvard College in 1754, the year his father explored the Coos country. He was first settled in the ministry at Newent, then a parish in Norwich, Conn., now the town of Lisbon, where he labored some years; but taking a dismission from that charge, he came to Newbury at thirty-six years of age. Through his instrumentality a church was gathered and organized in Newbury, in the fall of 1764, composed of members from both sides of the river. The two settlements united, also, in forming an ecclesiastical society, which union continued nearly twenty years.

We now enter upon the transactions and events of 1765. During this year, the settlements at Coos began to have some neighbors. One or two settlements were made at Bradford, Orford, Lyme, Thetford, Hanover, Lebanon, and Plymouth; but more of these hereafter.

On the 24th of January, 1765, the Rev. Mr. Powers received a call to take the spiritual charge of this newly constituted church and society in the wilderness. He gave his answer in the affirmative, February 1, 1765. They then voted that "the installment be on the last Wednesday of this instant, and voted, that the Reverend Messrs. Abner Bailey, Daniel Emerson, Joseph Emerson, Henry True, and Joseph Goodhue, with their churches, be a council for said installment. Voted, that Jacob Bailey, Esq., shall represent the town of Newbury at the council, which was voted to meet for said installment *down country where it is thought best.* Jacob Kent, Town Clerk.

There is, to us, some novelty in this vote for installment *somewhere* ; but the necessity of the case explains the whole affair. There were no ministers or churches in all the region, and they must go by their delegation until they found them. The ministers selected for the council belonged in Hollis and vicinity, and the Rev. Mr. Powers was installed at Hollis, February 27, 1765, as the title page to the sermon that was preached on the occasion showeth, which is as follows : —

" A Sermon preached at Hollis, February 27, 1765, at the Installation of the Rev. Peter Powers, A. M., for the towns of Newbury and Haverhill, at a Place called Coos, in the Province of New-hampshire. By Myself. Published at the desire of many who heard it, to whom it is humbly dedicated by the unworthy author. Then saith he to his servants, the wedding is ready,—Go ye therefore into the high ways, and as many as ye shall find, bid to the marriage. Matt. xxii : 8, 9. Portsmouth, in New-hampshire. Printed and sold by Daniel and Robert Fowle, 1765."

There is novelty in the circumstance of Mr. Powers' preaching his own installation sermon, but it was nothing uncommon at that day ; and there is room for doubt whether the moderns have made an improvement in this particular.

Mr. Powers' goods were brought from Charlestown

to Newbury upon the ice on the river, the last of February, by the people of Newbury and Haverhill; but the family did not arrive until April of that year.

A circumstance occurred on the journey with the goods, which gave rise to an anecdote which was rife among the old people, down to a late period. It has been related to me by persons belonging to several different towns. There was a man living in Newbury, and a member of the church, by the name of *Way*. He was an eccentric character, and would on some occasions speak unadvisedly, yet was a very friendly man and was neld in general esteem. He was one who volunteered his services to bring up the goods upon the ice. It was so late in February, that in some places, especially where tributaries came in, the ice was thin and brittle. They, however, made their way without serious difficulty, until they came to the mouth of Ompompanoosuc, at the north-east part of Norwich, where Way's sled broke through, and had like to have gone down, sled, team, Way and all. But by timely effort on the part of his travelling companions, they were all extricated. As soon as Way and his team reached firm footing, he turned around and surveyed the danger he had been in; and as he saw the waters boiling and eddying with a frightful aspect, he said to his companions, "That is a cursed hole." When the party had arrived at Newbury, and they were relating the trials and dangers of the way, some one mentioned what Mr. Way said of Ompompanoosuc. It was not long before this came to the ears of Mr. Powers, and he resolved to go, as his custom was in like cases, and have a conversation with Mr. Way, and admonish him, if he should be found to have been delinquent. He accordingly went and told Mr. Way that he had been told he had been speaking unadvisedly and wickedly. "What, what is it?" said Mr. Way. "Why, they say you said of Ompompanoosuc, that *it was a cursed hole.*" "Well, it *is* a cursed hole," said Way; "I say, it is a cursed hole, and I can prove it." "O no, you cannot," said Mr. Powers, "and you have done very wrong—you must repent." "Why," said Way, "did not the Lord curse the earth for man's sin?" "Yes," said Mr. Powers. "Well," replied Way, "do you think that little *divilish* Ompompanoosuc was an exception?" Mr. Powers turned away, and exclaimed, "O, Mr. Way, Mr. Way, I stand in fear of you," and recording his *nolle prosequi*, departed.

Mr. Powers lived in a house a little north of the house of Gen. Bailey, and south of Thomas Johnson's. He preached for a time at Gen. Bailey's house, and in the mean time, they built a log meeting-house, south of Gen. Bailey's, and north of the hill, where they worshipped some years. This was the house voted to be built, 28 feet by 25 feet, in October, 1764, as stated by the Rev. Mr. Perry in his manuscript of 1831, but which he concludes never was builded (pp. 14 and 16, in manuscript). The truth is, Mr. Perry was laboring under a mistake in regard to meeting-houses. The first meeting-house stood where I have located it. A framed meeting-house was some years afterward erected near where the present Congregational meeting-house stands; but as there was dissatisfaction in regard to its location, it was pulled down, and re-erected on the spot where Mr. Perry speaks of the first meeting-house standing, viz., "west of the burying ground;" but it was not for a meeting-house that it was erected there, but for a court-house and jail; still, divine service might have been maintained there after the first house had become too small to accommodate the congregation, and before the present meeting-house was erected in 1790.

I wish here to be indulged with a single remark in respect to Brother Perry's manuscript. It was a very laudable undertaking. I am not altogether unaided by it; but he was in too much haste in preparing it;

depended too much on common report, and did not compare notes sufficiently. It will not guide us safely through the labyrinth of the twenty-five first years in these settlements. But as I have said, they worshipped at the Ox Bow some years, and Haverhill people assembled with them, with great punctuality. There was a foot-path leading from Judge James Woodward's late residence, north-westerly, to the river, where was a log canoe to set them across, and from the point of landing a serpentine path through tall grass, bushes, and sometimes towering trees, led them to the place of worship. They had another canoe at the Dow farm, and another at the Porter place.

At that day it was a sin and disreputable in the view of all, for persons to absent themselves from the place of worship without valid cause ; and parents were seen uniformly carrying their children in their arms from Dr. Carleton's place to the Johnson Village and back again, the same day, and sometimes when the grass and bushes were wet, and the trees from above dropped upon them their dewy blessings ; and all this, that they might hear the word of life dispensed. Going and returning in their meandering course could not have been a less distance than twelve miles, and sometimes *each* parent had one to carry.

Nor was the attendance at worship less uniform and punctual with those on the west side of the river. Some females walked from Moretown, now Bradford, and others from Ryegate, a distance of ten miles. Those from the latter place, when they came to Well's River, (there being no canoe,) would bare their feet, and "trip it along as nimbly as the deer." The men generally went bare-footed; the ladies, certainly, wore shoes.

The wife of Judge Ladd related to me her extreme mortification on the first Sabbath she attended meeting at the Ox Bow. She and her husband had been recently married. They came from Haverhill, Mass., and had seen and tasted some of the refinements of life. She thought she must appear as well as any of them, and put on her wedding silks, with muffled cuffs, extending from the shoulder to the elbow, and there made fast by brilliant sleeve-buttons. (Ladies of the toilet of eighty years' experience will understand all this.) She wore silk hose and florid shoes. Her husband, appeared, also, in his best, and they took their seats on benches early in the sanctuary. But she remarked that "they went alone, sat alone, and returned alone; for it was not possible for her to get near enough to any one of the females to hold conversation with them; and she was so home-sick, she thought she should die, and would have given any thing could she have formed some acquaintance with those who were to be her female neighbors," but they were actually afraid of her, and each sat, or stood, at a proper distance, lest they should soil her dress. On their return home, she told her husband she had learned one lesson, and that was, *When among Romans, conform to Romans.* The next Sabbath she appeared in a clean check-linen gown, and other articles in accordance, and she found very sociable and warm-hearted friends.

But their worship was destined to interruptions in the summer of 1765. I have already spoken of Sam'l Sleeper, the first settler in Newbury, in 1762; that he was a Quaker preacher, and that he came on to take possession for Gen. Bailey. We do not hear of any irregularities practised by Sleeper until after the settlement of Mr. Powers. Then he claimed the right to hold forth at any time, and on all occasions, when the Spirit moved him; and while Mr. Powers was speaking, he would sometimes say—" Thee lies, friend Peter." And at other times he would vociferate— " False doctrines ! false doctrines ! " Then again— " Glorious truths ! glorious truths !" The principal men used all means to dissuade him from such a course of conduct ; but he grew more insolent and boisterous, and they at length incarcerated him in a cellar on Musquash Meadow; but as soon as Sleeper was disposed of, one Benoni Wright, a convert and pupil of Sleeper, volunteered to fill the vacated seat of his master, and if Sleeper had chastised the sinners with *whips*, Wright would do it with *scorpions*. He permitted his beard to grow at full length, and by this, he became a professed prophet of the Lord, and delivered his messages in the most boisterous and frantic manner. But he gained no converts, and as he resisted every remonstrance of the people, they adopted a summary course with him. The elders of the people in both settlements took him on to the meadow, near where Sleeper was in duress, held a court upon him, convicted him, and doomed him to receive "ten lashes, well laid on." Wright was stripped and received the judgment of the court upon the spot, and the same self-constituted court passed a decree, and sent it to Sleeper, that if he appeared again after confinement, to make the least disturbance, he should receive *thirty lashes* in full tale. This was decisive, and these prophets concluded to sacrifice their consciences at the shrine of their bodies. Peace and order were restored.

But the next season, 1766, Sleeper and Wright left the settlement in Newbury, and removed into Bradford, and settled on the meadow, north of Mr. Hunkins, and east of what was Johnson's tavern, in the north of Bradford. Here Wright undertook to sustain a fast of forty days, and withdrew to a cave in a mountain, at the north-west part of Bradford. And that he might gird himself for his conflict with hunger and the *Prince of the power of the air*, he procured him a strap with forty holes in it, and was to buckle himself up one hole each day; but long before he had attained to a "good degree," he was so pressed upon by hunger, that he concluded to return home to his wife, and get her to prepare him a good supper. She did so, and just as Wright was sitting down to his repast, in bolted Sleeper, who exclaimed, "Friend Wright, dost thou break thy fast?" Wright was moon-struck for a time ; but his appetite prevailed, and he returned not to the mountain, which has from that time borne his name, *Wright's Mountain*. From this time these two men wholly disappear from our history.

Col. Joshua Howard related to me in 1824, and confirmed the same in 1832, that the origin of Sleeper's opposition was this :—Gen. Bailey found it somewhat difficult to procure a man to come on and take possession of that land amidst the Indians, who would not like as well to take possession for himself, as for another; and such a man he did not want. He at length came across Sleeper, who promised he would go on, provided he might become their Quaker preacher, when they had obtained their grant, and had formed a Christian society. Bailey, willing to indulge his whim, said to him pleasantly, "O; yes, Sleeper, you shall be our minister." Sleeper took it all for specie, and in process of time, Bailey found there was more of Quakerism than poetry in Sleeper.

In the fall of this year, 1765, Judge Woodward was married to Hannah Clark, and it was the first marriage ceremony ever performed in the county of Grafton; and as there were some things attending it out of the ordinary course, and as I had the particulars from the judge himself, I will relate them, as they will serve to show that some things could be done then, as well as at this time. I have stated that Judge Woodward came into Haverhill in 1763, and bought his meadow farm. He built his first tent upon the meadow, as nearly all the first settlers did in Newbury, and some in Haverhill, not knowing that they would be in danger from floods; but being driven off by a flood in 1771, they afterwards built upon more elevated ground. But Woodward was now enjoying single blessedness in his tent. He felled trees by day, went to the Dow farm for his meals, and slept on the meadow at night. And although he sometimes dreamed of fairy forms, of sparkling eyes, and ruby lips, yet he knew not that Providence had any thing of this kind in reserve for him, and if he had, he knew not where it might be found ; for young females, in *those days*, were duly appreciated. But the next year, when Judge Ladd came on, he brought with him a blooming little maid, Hannah Clark, of fifteen, to live in his family a year or two, and then, in the mind of Judge Ladd and wife, she would become the wife of John Ladd, a brother of Judge Ladd. Woodward went to see his neighbor Ladd, and there he saw the object, which took, at once, full possession of his soul ; and he could not see why he might not enjoy it, as well as John Ladd ; and from that moment, he resolved to secure Hannah Clark for his wife, if it was in his power. He called at Judge Ladd's occasionally, and had some brief opportunities for conversation with Hannah, enough to satisfy him that his views and feelings were reciprocated, before Judge Ladd or his wife suspected the choice or intention of either ; but as soon as their suspicions were awakened, Woodward was prohibited the privilege of visiting at the house, and a strict watch was maintained over this little blushing girl. But after all, they had their friends, and billets, and flowers, and compliments passed between them; and occasionally an interview was obtained through the intervention of friends. This kind of innocent conspiracy was carried on against Judge Ladd and wife one full year, and then the parties thought seriously of deciding the controversy by a clandestine marriage. The plan was laid and executed in the following manner : —

Woodward went to Newbury, and told all his heart to Ephraim Bailey, son of Gen. Bailey, and brought him to espouse his cause, and to co-operate with him. Woodward told Bailey they must have one female enlisted in their interests. Bailey said he believed he could find one that would sustain that part. He was then paying his addresses to a young girl by the name of Hannah Fellows, and he could initiate her into the secret, and secure her aid. It was accordingly confided to her, and it was so arranged that Hannah Fellows was to pass over to Haverhill, and spend the afternoon in visiting Hannah Clark, tell her what was expected of her, and the sun about an hour high, she was to solicit the favor of Mrs. Ladd to have Hannah Clark walk with her as far as the river on her return to Newbury. In the mean time, the Rev. Mr. Powers was to be requested to be upon the west bank of the river precisely at such an hour, and Ephraim

Bailey was to set him across in the canoe, and then all were to step into Woodward's tent, and the marriage ceremony be performed. Woodward had already taken out license from under the king to authorize his being married without publishment, and every thing succeeded according to previous arrangement. The moment the two Hannahs came on to the meadow, Mr. Powers and Ephraim Bailey were seen coming up from the river. They all entered into Woodward's tent, and in a short time Woodward and Hannah Clark were joined in lawful marriage. Those who belonged to Newbury returned forthwith and Hannah Clark, now Hannah Woodward, ran for Judge Ladd's. She had not been absent long enough to excite suspicion in the mind of any one. Hannah continued to do for Judge Ladd as heretofore, and Woodward labored on the meadow.

At length, it was reported by Mr. Powers, that he had married Woodward to Hannah Clark, not knowing that there was any secret to be kept. After some little time, a woman came over to pay a visit to Mrs. Ladd, and told her what kind of a story was going the rounds in Newbury, that James Woodward was married to Hannah Clark. Mrs. Ladd told her, " There was not a word of truth in the story ; that Woodward had been endeavoring to court Hannah, but they would not hear to it." The woman replied, "It was a little extraordinary that such a story should be made from nothing, and she had understood that it came from Mr. Powers. And do you *know*," said she, "that it is not true?" "Why, yes," said she, "it cannot be true." At that moment she paused and reflected, as though Hannah's walk with Hannah Fellows had just streaked across her mental horizon. "But," said she, "if I don't know, I will," rising up at the same time, and making for the kitchen, where Hannah was carding wool or tow : "Hannah," said she, "they say you are married to James Woodward; is it true?" "Yes, ma'am," said Hannah. "Then I have nothing more for you to do," replied Mrs. Ladd; "I shall not part man and wife." Hannah put her cards together, laid them into her basket rose up, and ran for the meadow, and lived happily with her husband forty years, and departed this life Oct. 21, 1805. Hon. James Woodward livéd to the advanced age of eighty, and departed this life 1821.

I perceive that Thompson, in his Gazetteer of Vermont, states that the crank for the first saw-mill in Newbury was drawn upon a hand-sled from Concord, N. H., to Newbury, Vt. Distance seventy miles. I suppose it could not have been much less than seventy miles from Concord to Newbury, since it is seventy-two miles from Haverhill Corner direct to Concord. They would have been much nearer the true distance at that time, had they stated it at eighty miles. But the whole of this tour I have in minutes from the lips of two of the adventurers themselves, Judge Woodward and John Page. I do not know the precise number of men who went for the Irons, but I think as many as six. They prepared a rude hand sleigh, I do not recollect the technical name for it. They split a hard wood sapling, and shaved the two flat sides, as the cooper would do a hoop for a hogshead. The flat and wide side was the bottom of the runner, and it was bent up forward, and the end being shaved down small, it entered a hole in a thick ribbon; and the runner and ribbon were supported apart by studs entering the runner and ribbon, or nave, at short distances from each other, from end to end. The cross-bars rested upon the ribbons. This vehicle secured several advantages. It was light; the runners were wide, and would not readily cut through the snow; the beams were high from the ground, so that rocks and stubs were not likely to strike the cross-beams. Being thus equipped, they took in their provisions and set sail with light hearts. There was more sport, however, in going to

Concord with an empty sled, than in returning with a ponderous freight.

>...........facilis descensus Averni :
>Sed revocare gradum,...............
>Hoc opus, hic labor est.

The snow was deep, and it proved to be a very cold week, and before one half the distance was gained on their return voyage, they felt themselves exhausted by fatigue, and benumbed with the cold. They came through Hebron, and came on to Newfound Pond, because the way was more level, yet the cold more severe, for they had not the forest to break the force of the wind. Having gained somewhat more than mid way of the pond, which is six miles in length, they made a halt, and took their seats upon their sled for rest. Page arose and went some little distance to a glade, or opening in the ice, to drink, and when he returned, he found all his companions sinking down into a sleep, from which, if it had been indulged, no power short of Omnipotence could have aroused them. Page was not lost to a sense of *his* or *their* danger; the thought of which proved the necessary stimulus to excite him to effort in redeeming them from death. He cried out to them that they were all dead men, if they did not instantly awake, and bestir themselves. He seized them by their shoulders, shook them, and made them stand up; and he so preached terror to their auditory nerves, that they revived, and resolved to make every possible effort to reach a camp in the woods; and they were successful, and thus saved themselves alive.

I speak of their reaching a camp. It may be proper for me to state in this place, that our fathers had taken the precaution to build camps on the route from Haverhill to Salisbury, one camp in every twelve or fifteen miles, and each was supplied with fireworks and fuel, so that a traveller could soon kindle him a fire; and he had the boughs of the hemlock for his bed.

But this same party came near perishing when they had arrived in sight of Haverhill, in the north-east part of Piermont; and had it not been for Woodward to perform for Page, in that instance, what Page had done for them upon the pond, they would have given up the ghost. But they were told it required but one effort more, and all danger was past; but if they gave way to sleep for a few minutes, as one of them proposed, they never would awake in the body. They were induced to persevere, and they came into Haverhill, where they found the blessings of a fireside, of food, comfortable lodgings, and anxious friends to sympathize with them.

This saw-mill crank was the one which was so long in use at Atwood's mills in Newbury, but I know not its location or its use at this time. But what hardships were these above related! How unlike the condition of their children and grand-children! How unequal are their descendants to such services! Many of our young men would now groan under the task of travelling on foot from Haverhill to Plymouth, a distance of thirty-two miles, on a road which may be passed over in safety, by horse and carriage, at the rate of ten miles per hour. But the memory of one man will carry him back to a different generation. There he will see a hardy race, minds trained to deeds of daring, and muscular powers, seldom, if ever, surpassed. And these qualities did not appertain to the first settlers of Coos exclusively, but they characterized those several generations which felled our forests, subdued our soil, conquered savage men, destroyed the beasts of prey, made roads, built habitations, mills, school-houses, churches, supported the gospel, founded colleges and academies, sustained a war of eleven years with the combined forces of French and Indians, and finally gained our national independence. They had a great work assigned them, and Providence fitted them, in an eminent degree, for the discharge of their duties.

I will here mention, that roads direct from Haverhill to Boston were not opened until after the war of the revolution—I mean such as would admit the passing of heavy teams, and until then, the freight of goods from our seaports was very expensive. Heavy articles which were not brought up from Charlestown upon the ice, in winter, were brought on pack-horses from Concord through the woods, and ten bushels of wheat have been exchanged for one of salt. The glass for Col. Thomas Johnson's house was brought across the woods in this manner; and Col. Robert Johnson, who opened the first tavern in Newbury, in a house a little south of where his son Robert now lives, supplied his bar with spirits imported in the same way. This being the state of things in respect to roads, we shall readily conceive that the means of communicating between this isolated settlement and the eastern part of the state were very limited, and were not an every day occurrence. A passenger arriving in the settlement with packages direct from friends in the east created a more lively interest in the settlers, than the arrival of the British Queen steamer now does in the great emporium of this nation. I will give an anecdote from Mr. Perry's sketches, illustrative of the state of things in these respects. The story comes from Richard Chamberlain, one of the first settlers.

Early in the settlement of the Coos, it so happened that the annual Thanksgiving was passed, before intelligence of it arrived here. But soon after, a Dr. White came up to visit his friends at Newbury, and brought with him a proclamation. This proclamation was read publicly on the Sabbath by Mr. Powers, and by him it was proposed they should keep a thanksgiving, notwithstanding the time specified by the governor was passed. And he proposed the *next Thursday*. Upon this a member arose, and gravely proposed that it might be deferred longer; "for," said he, "there is not a drop of molasses in the town; and we know how important it is to have molasses to keep Thanksgiving. My boys have gone to No. 4, and will be back, probably, by the beginning of next week, and they will bring molasses; and it had better be put off till next week Thursday." It was unanimously agreed to. But the molasses not coming, it was deferred another week; and finally, Thanksgiving was kept without molasses. This, which is enough to provoke a smile, will nevertheless show us the simplicity and destitution of those days.

But from 1766 to 1769, we have no special occurrences to relate. The settlements continued to increase, society to improve, and the means of subsistence rewarded the hand of industry most bountifully. Indeed, the Coos meadows became to other infant settlements, north and south of them, what the granaries of Egypt were to Canaan and surrounding nations, in the days of the seven years' famine. An aged gentleman in Lyme, N. H., says, "he can very well recollect when they used to carry up their silver shoe-buckles to the Coos, and exchange them for wheat."

As to the state of religion in those years, we do not learn of any powerful revivals among the people, such as had been experienced in Whitfield's time, in many parts of New England ; or such as have since been experienced in those settlements. There are no church records to guide our bark in these polar seas ; but if there were revivals, in the modern sense of the term, the *ancients* would have told us of them. There were additions to the church from time to time, from both sides of the river, until it consisted of a goodly number of members. The Rev. Mr. Powers was a serious, godly man, and more distinguished, I should think,. for his plain, faithful, and pungent preaching, than for grace in style or diction. He preached mostly without notes, and yet he generally studied his sermons. Those I have seen in print exhibit thought, arrangement, a deep knowledge of the Scriptures, and a soul full of the love of Christ and of the souls of men. His labors were abundant. As there were no ministers north of Charlestown, for some years after Mr. Powers settled at Coos, he was frequently called to attend funerals, weddings, and to preach lectures at infant settlements upon the river. Until there was a foot-path marked out upon the bank of the river for passengers, Mr. Powers used to perform his journeys up and down the river in his canoe. When he saw young men felling trees near the river, he would call to them, and say, if Providence favored him, he would preach to them in that place, on such a day, and at such an hour. These were welcome propositions, generally; and if there were other settlements near, they were informed of the appointment; and Mr. Powers, at the hour specified, would find his hearers seated on stumps and logs, all ready to receive the word. Mr. Powers was characterized by his punctuality in meeting his appointments, and seldom, if ever disappointed his assembly.

John Mann, Esq., of Orford, told me that Mr. Powers passed down the river at a certain time, and gave out an appointment to preach at a particular hour, on a subsequent day. But during his absence, there fell a great rain, which swelled the river, and increased the rapidity of the current very much.

The people generally felt that he could not meet his appointment; but they assembled notwithstanding, and waited to know the result. One man was very confident Mr. Powers would not, and *could* not return, and was disposed to charge their assembling to a stupid credulity in the people. But another man seemed to be confident he would return to his appointment; and, finally, a bet was made between them. Neither one was pious. This altercation had awakened some interest in the audience generally, and all eyes were directed down the river. The appointed hour now drew on, and not more than twenty-five or thirty minutes remained in which Mr. Powers could make good his appointment, and he who bet against his return felt sure of his prize, for, if he was already in sight, he could not gain the ground within the time allotted; but more than this, no man or boat appeared in the river. But while all were anxious, and looking, the boat, on a sudden, rode into full view, as by magic, and not half the distance from them as was the spot on which their eyes were fixed. He had kept so near the shore next to them, to avoid the force of the current, that they could not see him until he threw his boat into the stream to pass an obstruction; and when he did appear so suddenly and so near, the assembly could not suppress their surprise and gladness, but welcomed him with a shout which rebounded from hill to valley. Mr. Powers stood before them at the appointed moment.

Col. Otis Freeman, of Hanover, related to me the particulars of the first marriage ceremony that was ever performed in that town. It was in 1767, and Mr. Powers officiated. Col. Otis Freeman attended the wedding. A transient man came into the town of Hanover, by the name of Walbridge, and made suit to Hannah Smith, daughter of a Mr. Smith, who lived on the place which Timothy Smith improved some years ago, and, for aught I know, does at this time. The parents of Hannah were very much averse to their daughter's connection with that man; but she resolved, and *so was resolved*. Walbridge happened to see Mr. Powers one day descending the river in his canoe, and he hailed him, and desired to know if he could return by such a day, and marry him at the house of Mr. Smith. Mr. Powers said he would do so, if Providence prospered him. He accordingly appeared at the house a little after sunset; the guests were assembled; the house being lighted up, the couple presented themselves, handed in their certificate, and wished Mr. Powers to proceed.

It was Mr. Powers' practice to call on the parents

of the candidates for marriage to know if they had aught to object to the marriage; and when, in this case, he called for the parents of the bride, behold, they were not there! Mr. Powers wished to know if they were not living. "Yes, they were living they supposed." He asked, if they were not in town. "They supposed they were; but they did not know." "How long since they were seen here?" "Just at night?" "Are the parents averse to this marriage?" "They supposed they were, some." "Could they not be brought to attend there that night?" If they could not, he should not proceed to the marriage ceremony that night. This was an unpleasant predicament for all parties. But a lantern or a torch was found, and a scout was sent forth in search of the old folks. They were found at the nearest neighbors, which was not very near, and after much persuasion, they were prevailed on to return home.

All parties were by this time cool and collected. The parents took their seats in the middle of the room, between the minister and the anxious couple. Mr. Powers arose, and addressing himself to the parents, said, "Is this young lady your daughter?" They bowed assent. "Are you willing I should proceed to join this couple in marriage?" The father fixed his eyes full on Mr. Powers some time, and a dead silence reigned, until Freeman saw the tears swelling in the old man's eyes, and his chin shook like an aspen leaf, and then came a sudden and convulsive response—" *Yeâ!* " which electrified the whole of them. the *a* in *yea* was sounded as broad as â in *hâll*, and the *e* not sounded at all. All sympathized with the old people, and Mr. Powers could scarcely proceed with the ceremony; but it was performed, and the connection proved an unhappy one. Walbridge was a worthless character. But this was the first marriage in Hanover, as Judge Woodward's was the first in Haverhill—the results widely different.

Mr. Powers being thus known, and being generally loved and respected, did much to increase the settlement at Coos. Persons often attended worship there from Thetford, Orford, Bradford, and Piermont. There was one Deacon Howard, who lived near the river in Thetford, who used to ride to Newbury often with his wife to hear Mr. Powers, and he loved him as his own soul.

At this time there were no taverns between Charlestown and Coos, and adventurers were necessitated to stop at such houses as they could find for refreshment and lodgings. They had called on this Deacon Howard, some making him compensation, and some not, until his means for subsistence were running low ; and he had resolved that it was not his duty to entertain any more strangers ; and this he could do more conscientiously, as there was a sort of an inn opened for their accommodation three miles north of him.

Mr. Powers, at a certain time, passed down the river on horseback, undiscovered by the deacon, and as he was on his return home, he found he should be overtaken by the darkness of night before he could reach the inn, and as it began to rain just before he came to Deacon Howard's, he thought he would there stop and spend the night. He accordingly rode up to the door, in the dusk of the evening, and tapped with his whip upon the door. The deacon came to the door, and asked what he wished for. Mr. Powers replied, that he was journeying up the river ; that he was overtaken by the night and by rain ; and he should like to put up with him for the night. The deacon answered in an abrupt and gruff tone of voice, " I cannot keep you. Folks have come here until they have eaten me out of house and home, and we cannot consent to take you in." Mr. Powers replied that he was much fatigued, and he knew not how to proceed farther ; he would pay him whatever he was disposed to charge him. " No," said the deacon, " I cannot keep you. There is a house for en-

4*

tertainment three miles ahead, and you *must* go there."

By this time, the old lady had come forward, and was looking over her husband's shoulder, listening to the conversation as it proceeded; and as Mr. Powers began to turn his horse away from the door, she said to her husband, "It seems to me, that man speaks like Mr. Powers of Newbury." "Mr. Powers! no, he don't," said he. "But why don't you ask him who he is?" said she. "I don't *care* who he is," said he; "I can't keep him;" but, at the same time, stepping from his door, and advancing along after Mr. Powers, he said, "Where are you from, sir?" "Newbury," replied Mr. Powers. "From, *Newbury?*" "Yes, sir." "Well, you know the Rev. Mr. Powers, then, don't you?" "Yes, very well." "And he is a very good man, aint he?" "Some have a good opinion of him," said Mr. Powers, "much better than I have." "Well, you may go along."

By this time, the old lady had come up to her husband in the rain, and as the deacon was turning to go into the house, she said, "Husband, I *verily* believe that is Mr. Powers." On hearing this, he turned suddenly on his heel, and making rapid strides after the stranger, he cried out, "Sir, what is your *name?*"

"My name is Powers," was the reply. "You *rascal!*" exclaimed the deacon; and seizing him by one leg, drew him from his horse, held him fast until he got him into the house, and there he made all concessions to the man whom he loved above all others. A very happy interview they had of it, and the deacon continued to relate the particulars of this adventure with peculiar emotions until the close of life. He related them to Dr. Burton, and the doctor to myself.

Mr. Powers spent nearly twenty years at Newbury and Haverhill, and with the exception of the troubles which grew out of the revolutionary war, I believe their union was a happy and prosperous one.

Mr. Powers was a high whig, and by his preaching and efforts for the common cause of the colonies, he drew upon him the fierce resentment of the tories, and they threatened his life, which induced him to remove over into Haverhill, in the spring of 1781. This displeased many of his friends in Newbury, and although he continued to preach in Newbury one half the time, for a year or two, yet it resulted in his dismission from the church in Newbury, some time in 1782. But he preached still a year or two in Haverhill, and sometimes in Newbury, to particular friends; but he finally left, and went and settled on

Deer Isle, Me., where he closed his labors by his decease in May, 1800, aged 72. He died of a cancer. When told by his son Jonathan, who was then a settled minister at Penobscot, Me., that he was dying, he looked around on his family, and replied, "The will of the Lord be done," and yielded up the ghost. Mrs. Powers was Martha Hale, of Sutton, Mass. She was an intelligent, pious, and superior woman. She survived her husband until January, 1802, and died suddenly while on a visit to her children in Newbury.

To those who sat under the ministry of Mr. Powers, of whom there are some still living, and those who have looked upon him as their spiritual father, it will be pleasing to learn by what means their minister was prepared to preach to them the unsearchable riches of Christ. The facts which I shall here record I received from an eye and ear witness of what she related. It was the sister of the Rev. Peter Powers.

I have already related that Mr. Powers was the oldest child of Capt. Peter Powers and Anna, his wife; that they were the first settlers in the town of Hollis. I now relate that for about two years their nearest neighbor was at the travelling distance of ten miles, and this solitary family sustained all the privations and hardships which were incident to pioneers in these New England settlements. For about twelve years they had neither schools, or a preached gospel ; but they carried with them the Holy Scriptures and the love of God in their hearts. · Their children were instructed in the principles of the gospel, and they witnessed the blessedness of godliness in the daily walk of their parents. At an early age Peter became a devoted child of the Lord Jesus, and was endeared to his parents by a thousand ties ; for they looked to him as their first helper, under God, and fondly hoped he would be their support and solace in old age. But as Peter grew in years, a flame was kindled in his breast which could neither be extinguished nor suppressed ; and his parents often heard him say, "He had an ardent desire to enjoy the advantages of an academic and a collegiate education." But as these seemed altogether incompatible with their circumstances, and militated against all their previous arrangements, those desires of the son were treated by the parents as visionary ; and inadmissible, and for a time no human ear was offended by the importunities of the son ; and the parents hoped that the subject was relinquished and forgotten by him, until it was revived to them in the following manner :—

These parents were of Puritan strictness in the government of their family, and neither their sons nor their daughters were allowed in ordinary cases to be absent from the family at nine o'clock in the evening, which was the hour of prayer. But it appeared on a calm summer's evening that Peter was absent at the hour of prayer; nor did he appear when it was necessary to close and secure the house against the intrusion of the Indians. The parents passed the night in agitation of spirits. At one moment, they trembled in view of his having fallen a victim to Indian treachery and violence, and their imaginations presented him pierced and lacerated upon the ground, or hurried away into a captivity more appalling than death. At another time they were vexed with the apprehension that their son had for the first time absented himself in wanton disregard of their views and feelings. The night was at length spent, and the father rose at the dawn of day; and as he unbarred the door, he saw his young son emerging from the forest, and approaching the dwelling with a solemn and down-cast look. The father beheld his son with the mixed emotion of joy and resentment;—*joy*, because he had received him safe and sound—*resentment* because he supposed there could be no adequate cause to justify the elopement; yet he restrained himself and called for no explanation until the hour of prayer when he was accustomed to administer reproof, if it was necessary. The family being seated, and a portion of Scripture having been read, the father paused, and fixing a reproving look upon Peter, said, "Where did you spend the night, Peter?" The son was exceedingly embarrassed, and did not return a prompt and explicit answer. The father more sternly repeats, "Peter, where did you spend the night?" The son faintly and meekly replied, while the tears coursed down his cheeks, "I spent it in the woods, sir." "In the *woods?*" said the father; *how* did you spend it?" "In prayer, sir." A pause of a moment succeeded, and the subdued soul of the father rushed to the eye, to seek the relief which utterance now denied. But soon the father resumed the inquiry, and, in an altered and subdued tone, said, "My son, what were you praying for, during the night?" "That I might go to college." "What would you go to college for, Peter?" "That I might be prepared to preach the gospel to sinners." The father turned and looked upon Anna, his wife in the deepest emotion, but could not speak. As soon as he possessed the power of utterance, he led in devotion, and as soon as Peter had gone out, the father said to Anna, in a soft and tremulous voice,

"I do not see but we must give up the matter, and let Peter go to college." The result was a collegiate course, a life of eminent usefulness, a triumphant death, and that eternal reward which is promised to those who turn many to righteousness.

Mr. Powers' dismission from Newbury church was the first step towards a dissolution of the union between Haverhill and Newbury in all ecclesiastical concerns; and it does not appear that they ever assisted each other in supporting the gospel afterwards. And the probability is each town was beginning to feel itself able to support preaching independent of the other. We find a proposition coming from Mr. Powers to Newbury church and society, so early as December, 1781, "for an agreement between the town of Haverhill and the town of Newbury to be separate parishes." This proposition was undoubtedly from the people of Haverhill, and therefore we find a vote of Newbury, December 31, 1781, "That the above committee treat with the town of Haverhill, relative to the Rev. Peter Powers." They also vote to make a settlement with Mr. Powers for all arrearages. Mr. Samuel Powers, of Newbury, son of the Rev. Peter Powers, and a very worthy citizen, says, "he can well remember the time of his father's dismission from Newbury; that Newbury church did not unite in the council for his dismission, and the council sat in Haverhill." But the church in Haverhill was not constituted a separate church until some years after the sitting of this council, an event to be noticed hereafter.

I will in this place relate an extraordinary case of instinct in a cow, as related to me by Capt. Howard, and I relate it *here*, before I proceed to the events of 1769, because it occurred in the first years of these settlements. Col. John Hurd came into Haverhill at an early period of the settlement, from Portsmouth, and lived a little north of Moses Southard's, or the old Porter place, at Horse Meadow. He came first to Charlestown, and then up the river, as most others did. With him he brought a valuable cow, which he turned upon the meadow, where, for aught that appeared, she was well content to abide ; but, after a lapse of a few weeks, the cow was on a sudden among the missing, and nothing could be found of her. They went through both settlements, and searched in vain ; no one had seen her. The colonel then employed Indian runners to go in pursuit of her; they were out one full week, and returned without her, but reported that they had been on her trail in Coventry ; but east of that, they could discover no trace of her. Hurd gave her up as lost. But the next autumn, there came a man from Portsmouth, bearing letters from friends, and in one of them it was stated that on such a morning, the *old cow* was found in the barn-yard from which she took her departure some months before. She was in good keeping. Now, we must consider, that from Portsmouth to Charlestown is at this day, in the most direct route, ninety-six miles; from Charlestown to Horse Meadow nearly seventy miles; and from Horse Meadow to Portsmouth cannot be less than one hundred miles, for it is the hypotenuse of the triangle, which has Portsmouth, Charlestown, and Haverhill for its angles. The cow unquestionably travelled all three sides of the triangle; and what seems most surprising is, that after travelling more than one hundred miles, as the roads then were, north of west, and much of that distance was woods, then more than seventy miles east of north, all woods, the cow should have kept in her mind the direct bearing of Portsmouth, and that she should have made the journey from Haverhill to Portsmouth, an entire wilderness, and have reached her old home in safety, without guide or protector. She might have fallen in with Barrington or Stratford, twenty miles north-west of Portsmouth, but she did not do it, probably, or she would have been taken up; yet she performed her tour, and gained her destination.

I now come to speak of events of 1769, and onward. It was in April, of this year, that Col. Chas. Johnston came into Haverhill, and settled at the Corner. Col. Johnston was born at Hampstead, N. H., 1737. He married Ruth Marsh, of Londonderry, N. H., and came to Haverhill at thirty-two years of age.

Col. Johnston had departed this life prior to my coming to Haverhill, and I am wholly dependent upon others for the information I have respecting him. But no man's character could be better established in the public mind, and seldom can we find greater unanimity with the public in bestowing on one man the meed of commendation. There is still a blessed savor of him remaining in Haverhill and vicinity.

I am in possession of an interesting occurrence which took place on the journey of Col. Charles and his family from Hampstead to Haverhill. I have it in the hand-writing of Mr. Richard Wallace, of Thetford, Vt., who was born in Nova Scotia, in 1753, and at the age of sixteen years accompanied Mr. Johnston to Haverhill, I shall give it in his own words, with the correction of some errors in orthography and grammatical construction of sentences. Mr. Wallace's early opportunities for an education were limited, as nearly all were at that day ; but he sustained a character above suspicion for veracity, and had been a professed disciple of Christ many years when he wrote me this statement. He says:—

"On the second day's journey from Hampstead, N. H., (this was in April, 1769, in the afternoon of this day) my feet became tender and swollen, and much parboiled, as was the common phrase at that day. This caused me to fall in the rear of the family many rods. I then concluded I would take off my shoes and stockings, and travel bare-footed, expecting by this means to be able to overtake the family. But my feet being swollen, and stockings wet, I was hindered in drawing them a good while, and I fell far in the rear. I then hastened my steps forward as fast as I could, the sun being about a half an hour high at night, as near as I can recollect. After wading a large brook, I entered the *eleven-mile-woods*, for the first time, in the upper part of Boscawen. I had not travelled far before I came to ice in the sled road, both in the middle and at the side, although the snow was for the most part gone in the woods. But I made all the speed I could, till it was almost dark, when I came to a brook or stream, that I dared not attempt to ford without daylight, nor could I find any tree fallen across the stream, on which I might pass over. But concluding I must stay there for the night, I went in immediate search of a convenient place to rest. I soon found a large tree fallen on the side of a knoll, the butt end lying up from the ground, leaving just room enough for me to crawl under. I took my long stockings, and drew the dry part of them on to my feet, and crawled under the tree, and being very tired, I soon fell asleep; and I think it likely I slept two or three hours, or more—I cannot tell exactly. But my anxiety did not leave me when asleep; and when I awoke, I was very cold, as there was a hard frost that night. Besides this, I found myself saluted from all parts of the solitary and dreary wilderness, by all the animal inhabitants of the forest, like a band of instrumental music, the wolves taking the chief lead, and carrying the highest notes; or something like a bass-viol and bassoon in their different strains. They did not appear to be far off, but did not come near me to offer any violence; yet their noise was some alarming, and very disagreeable, since the whole region of the forest seemed to be alive with these different kinds of animals. By and by, somebody cried out over my head, and barked like a little dog, then again screamed in the voice of women, and laughed out like parrots. I had not learned their grammar, nor to raise and fall their notes, for I was but a boy from the sea coast, and had never heard the like before. But I thought I would not make any disturbance with them, if they would let me alone until morning. But as soon as morning appeared, I crawled out from under the tree, and suddenly screamed with all my might, "Stop your noise!" I was immediately obeyed. And behold, the noisy creatures over my head were no other than great owls, roosting upon a branch of a tree! But I soon made ready to decamp, though my shoes and stockings were so frozen, that I could only get on my shoes slipshod. After some search, I found a log which enabled me to get over the brook, and I found the road, and I walked and ran as I could, some miles, and I reached Favor's tavern in New-Chester, that now is, just as the sun arose. Some of the company were up, and some getting up, and friends never came together in greater joy. I never shall forget how Col. Charles looked when he told me what concern he had had for me through the night.

"RICHARD WALLACE."

I would, in conclusion of this narration, raise the inquiry of those youth of sixteen, into whose hands the above statement may come, whether *they* would covet such a night's rest; and whether such a serenade from the beasts of the wilderness would be to them "some alarming, and very disagreeable!"

When Col. Johnston arrived at Haverhill, he purchased the ground where Haverhill Corner now is, and located himself on the ground where Capt. Powers pitched his camp for the night, in July, 1754, and wrote in his journal—" Here was the best of upland, and some quantity of large white pines."

I had it from the widow of Col. Johnston, who survived the death of her husband several years, and died, in 1816, at the age of seventy-five, that when they came to Haverhill, and found themselves hemmed in on every side by those towering trees and a dense underwood, she became very much discontented, and endured for some time all the melancholy and depression which arise from *home-sickness.* When suffering from the strongest paroxysms of this malady, she would sometimes go out to her husband, while he was felling trees upon what is now the common, and relate her distresses to him, in hopes that he might be induced to relinquish his hold on Coos, and return to their friends at the east. But the colonel, to amuse her, and to dissipate her melancholy would seat her upon a large stump, and then begin to describe to her the future village which they should ere long witness in that place. "On such a line would be the main street; on such a spot the court-house would stand; the academy would occupy such a site, and the meeting-house stand *there!*" For the moment, she would seem to fancy it a reality; but the next sober thought would dissipate her relief, and she would exclaim, "Mr. Johnston, there can't be any such thing! I know there can't. It never will be in this world!"

It is probable that the colonel thought as little of this ever being realized by them as she did; and yet both lived to witness, almost to a jot and tittle, those very predictions fulfilled. And no man in that town ever contributed more towards converting that wilderness into a delightful village than Col. Johnston. He was laborious and prudent, yet generous and brave. He accumulated a handsome estate; and by his beneficence, he often caused the poor, the widow, and the fatherless to sing for joy, and their blessings came upon him.

He was a man of great muscular powers, and he often put them forth, not to foment quarrels and broils, as is often the case in a rude state of society, but to suppress outbreakings and fightings; and those who were acquainted with him, refrained from those hostile attacks in his presence, for they knew the colonel would immediately stand between the parties, the advocate of peace and good order.

It is related of him that he was passing the inn at

the Corner, at a certain time, just when two strangers, who had met there, fell into a violent contention, and came to blows. The encounter was sharp and bloody; but, as the colonel's custom was, he walked up to the combatants, and placing his hands gently upon their shoulders, began to expostulate with them in the kindest manner, when they mutually left beating each other, and commenced dealing blows at him, who would have set them as one again. Upon this, the colonel held one in each hand firmly by the shoulder, and suddenly extending his arms to the right and left, he threw the assailants apart, but brought them again in contact, face to face, in front of him, with such power, that before this was repeated the third time, they called out for quarter, nor did he let go of them until they promised to be at peace with each other.

It was said in his day, and is said to this day, that Col. Johnston was a peace-maker, both in church and state. I have one instance of this, given by Mr. Wallace, who lived with the colonel after they came to Haverhill. He says, in a letter bearing date December 25, 1828, "Esquire Charles was the only justice of the peace in Haverhill prior to 1773. I will relate one anecdote of him in honor to his memory, and for a pious example for his descendants and others. Soon after his appointment for justice of the peace, there came a man to him with an earnest request for a writ against one of his neighbors. Esquire Johnston put him off by relating to him the unhappy consequences of neighbors going to law with each other; and recommended that he should go home and see his neighbor in a subdued temper of mind, and see if he would not pay him. The man went away, but soon returned with a bitter complaint and demanded a *writ*. The colonel left his business, called for his horse to be saddled, and said to the man, 'I am going with you to see if this matter cannot be settled without expense and strife.' When they came to the man so much complained of, the colonel told him his business, and that he came for the sake of peace. The man told him he was ready to settle the account, and always had been; and before they separated, all matters were adjusted, and the men parted in friendship." How much expense and strife might be avoided annually, if all our magistrates were of the same stamp! We say, "Blessed are the peace-makers."

I have another anecdote of the colonel, related to me by Esquire Jonathan Hale, of Coventry, N. H., who was knowing to the story. A poor man of Coventry bought a cow of Col. Johnston upon credit.

The cow was the principal support of the family; but after she had been kept through the winter, she sickened and died at the opening of spring. The man was distressed in view of the wants of his family, for he saw no way of relief. He knew it would be next to impossible for him to purchase a cow at that season, as it was generally known that he was still owing for the cow that he had lost; and he had nothing to pay for that, or another. He felt that he could not go to Col. Johnston for another, while he was still owing him for the first; but as it is said, "Hunger will break through a stone wall," so the distresses of his family impelled him to return to Col. Charles, as he was the only man living who inspired him with a gleam of hope. He went, and found the colonel at labor in his field. He related to him his disaster, and his distresses. The colonel sympathized with him deeply, and knew not what he could do. The poor man then told him his object in visiting him, which was to see if he could not obtain another cow of him. The colonel told him, "He did not see how he could supply him, for they had but two cows that season, and they were going to building, must have an unusual number of laborers, and they should need all that could be afforded by two cows." The poor man replied, "I did not come to you, colonel, with this request, supposing that you could relieve me without great inconvenience to yourself, and a sacrifice of interest, yet I was emboldened to make known my necessity."

The colonel paused in silence for a time, and manifested that there was a deep conflict between his sympathies and his circumstances. At length he said, "I will go to the house and see what Mrs. Johnston says." They went to the house, and the colonel related to his wife what had befallen the man, and what was his present object. Mrs. Johnston very naturally exclaimed, "You are not a going to let one of our cows go, are you?" And here she related what a demand they would have that season for both cows. The colonel heard her through patiently, and then said, "Do you not think that we can do better with one cow than this poor man can do, with his young children, without any?" Mrs. Johnston was silent. The colonel turned to the man, and said, "You will take my cow."

The poor man took his cow, and returned joyously with her to his family. How blessed is fellow-feeling! and still more blessed, when it is cherished by true piety and benevolence! If I know my own heart, I would rather have this written of my son than leave him in possession of the most splendid crown in

Europe. I have wondered a thousand times, and still wonder, why men of wealth do not secure to themselves, more frequently than they do, the happiness which Col. Johnston experienced in sending that man home with a light and grateful heart. We have no means of knowing whether that poor man was ever able to remunerate the colonel or not. No matter. If *he* did not, the *Lord* has done it, a thousand fold, and *verily, there is a reward for the righteous.*

I have spoken of the extraordinary muscular powers of Col. Johnston. I must relate one more event of his life, illustrative both of his physical power and of his courage. At the time when the New Hampshire troops signalized themselves at the battle of Bennington, under Gen. Stark, Col. Johnston was there, and sustained a part in the brilliant achievements of that ever-memorable day. After Col. Baum had surrendered to the American troops, and the battle was renewed by the arrival of Col. Breyman, Col. Johnston, in obedience to orders from Gen. Stark, was necessitated to pass through a narrow strip of woods on foot and alone, to bear some orders to another division of the American army. He had no weapon of defence but a stout staff, which he had cut in the woods that day, as he was passing on to Bennington from New Hampshire. Thus equipped, he came suddenly upon a British scout, in ambush, placed there to intercept communications between the different divisions of the Americans. The party in ambush was commanded by a Hessian lieutenant. As Johnston came up, this officer stepped forth, sword in hand, and claimed him as his prisoner. The word was no more than uttered, before the sword was struck from the hand of the officer by Johnston's staff, and as soon did Johnston have possession of that sword, and pointing it at the breast of the Hessian, declared to him, that he was that moment a dead man, if he and his party did not throw down their arms. The officer turned to his men and said, "We are prisoners of war." The soldiers threw down their arms, and Johnston marched them before him to the American lines, where they were received by our troops.

The colonel returned with the sword to his family, and presenting it to his only son, Capt. Michael Johnston, now of Haverhill, said, "This sword was won by valor—let it never be retaken through cowardice." The sword I have seen. It was a splendid article of the kind. There was a good deal of writing upon it, formed by etching, and the officer's name, which I do not now recollect. This sword, I have been told, was brought forth and exhibited for the mournful gratification of spectators on the day of the colonel's funeral solemnities. I am told that it was the colonel's expressed wish, before his death, that that sword might descend from him in the line of the oldest male heir, and that it has already gone into the possession of the Rev. Charles Johnston, of the town of Locke, Cayuga County, N. Y.

Col. Johnston was the first captain in the town of Haverhill; was for many years a justice of the peace; a colonel, a representative of the town many years; a judge of probate, and a deacon in the church. Col. Johnston's house was surrounded by a fort at Haverhill Corner, during the revolutionary war, as was Judge Ladd's, a little north of the old meeting-house, on Ladd street; also, Capt. Timothy Barns', who lived near the tavern, opposite the meeting-house, in the north parish in Haverhill. Col. Johnston departed this life, March 5, 1813, aged seventy-six.

In the summer of 1770, this whole section of country was visited by an extraordinary calamity, such a one as this country never experienced before or since, beyond what I shall here specify. It was an army of worms, which extended from Lancaster, N. H., to Northfield, in Massachusetts. They began to appear the latter part of July, 1770, and continued their ravages until September. The inhabitants denominated them the "Northern Army," as they seemed to advance from the north-west, and to pass east and south, although I do not learn that they ever passed the high lands between the Connecticut and Merrimack Rivers. They were altogether innumerable for multitude. Dr. Burton, of Thetford, Vt., told me that he had seen whole pastures so covered that he could not put down his finger in a single spot, without placing it upon a worm. He said, he had seen more than ten bushels in a heap. They were unlike any thing which the present generation have ever seen. There was a stripe upon the back like black velvet: on either side a yellow stripe from end to end; and the rest of the body was brown. They were sometimes seen not larger than a pin; but in their maturity, they were as long as a man's finger, and proportionably large in circumference. They appeared to be in great haste except when they halted to devour their food. They filled the houses of the inhabitants, and entered their kneading-troughs, as did the frogs in Egypt. They would go up the side of a house, and over it, in such a compact column, that nothing of boards or shingles could be seen! They did not take hold of the pumpkin-vine, peas, potatoes, or flax; but wheat and corn disappeared before them as by magic. They would climb up the stalks of wheat, eat off the stalk just below the head, and almost as soon as the head had fallen upon the ground, it was devoured. To prevent this, the men would "draw the rope," as they termed it; that is, two men would take a rope, one at each end, and pulling from each other until it was nearly straightened, they would then pass through their wheat fields, and brush off the worms from the stalks, and by perpetual action they retarded the destruction of their wheat; but it was doomed, finally, to extinction.

There were fields of corn on the meadows in Haverhill and Newbury standing so thick, large and tall, that in some instances it was difficult to see a man standing more than one rod in the field from the outermost row; but in ten days from the first appearing of the Northern Army, nothing remained of this corn but the bare stalks! Every expedient was resorted to by the inhabitants to protect their fields of corn, but all in vain. In the first place, they dug trenches around their fields, a foot and a half deep, hoping this might prove a defence; but they soon filled the ditch, and the millions that were in the rear went over on the backs of their fellows in the trench, and took possession of the interdicted food.

The inhabitants then adopted another expedient to save those fields yet standing. They cut a trench as before; then took round and smooth sapling sticks, of six or eight inches in diameter, and six or eight feet in length, sharpened them to a point, and with these made holes in the bottom of the ditch, once in two or three feet; and, as their meadows were bottom lands, they experienced no difficulty in extending these holes to two and three feet in depth, below the bottom of the trench. The sides of these holes were made smooth by the bar or lever which made the holes, and as soon as the worm stepped from the precipice, he landed at the bottom, and could not ascend again; indeed, he was soon buried alive by his unfortunate fellows, who succeeded him in his downfall. Now, those who made these holes to entrap their invaders, went around their fields, and plunged these pointed levers into the holes filled with worms, and destroyed every one of them at a single thrust, whether it was a peck or half a bushel. By unremitting effort in this way, some reserved to themselves corn enough for seed the next year.

About the first of September, the worms suddenly disappeared; and where they terminated their earthly career is unknown, for not the carcass of a worm was seen. In just eleven years afterward, in 1781, the same kind of worm appeared again, and the fears of the people were much excited; but they were comparatively few in number, and no one of the kind has ever been seen since.

This visitation, which destroyed the principal grains of that year, was felt severely by all the new settlements; for it not only cut off their bread-stuffs, but it deprived them of the means of making their pork to a great degree, and reduced the quantity of fodder for their cattle. The settlements at Haverhill and Newbury did not feel this calamity quite so much as those infant settlements in the towns north and south of them. They had been longer in their settlements, had some old stock of provisions on hand, and had more means to procure supplies from Charlestown, or by the *way* of Charlestown. Jonathan Tyler, of Piermont, related to me, that the settlements in that town were left without the means of subsistence from their own farms. His father drew hay on a hand sled upon the ice, from the great Ox Bow in Newbury, to support his cow the following winter. And had it not been for two sources opened for their support, they must have deserted the town. One was the extraordinary crop of pumpkins in Haverhill and Newbury. The corn being cut off, and the pumpkins remaining untouched by the Northern Army, they grew astonishingly, and seemed to cover the whole ground where the corn had stood, and the yield was great.

The people of Haverhill and Newbury gave the settlers in Piermont the privilege of carrying away, gratis, as many pumpkins as they would. They went up, made a kind of raft and transported them by water to Piermont. Their raft was a novelty in its kind, and will show us how truly " necessity is the mother of invention." They cut them two straight trees from forty to fifty feet in length, and from fifteen to eighteen inches in diameter ; and enough of these were generally found, already felled and dry, to answer their purpose. They bored holes near the ends of these trees, and introduced slats to hold them together at each end, in the manner that the long body of a hay-cart is made, only at twice or thrice the distance from each other that the sides of a hay-cart are placed. These two sides were first placed in the water, and then joined together. The pumpkins were then brought from the fields, which were contiguous to the river, and placed in the water, in this oblong square, until it was filled ; the pumpkins, being buoyant, would not sink, and could not escape from their pen. Two men in a skiff would then weigh anchor, and tow the raft of tons' weight to Piermont shores, where the freight was landed, and conveyed to the habitations of men !

Another source of support was opened to them in

the immense number of pigeons which Providence sent them immediately upon the disappearance of the Northern Army. Nothing could equal their number, unless it was the worms which had preceded them. The Tylers of Piermont, Daniel, David, and Jonathan, commenced taking pigeons on the meadow, west of Haverhill Corner, and in the space of ten days, they had taken more than four hundred dozen! They carried them to Piermont, and made what is defined, in the Yankee vocabulary, "a bee," for picking pigeons; and two or three times a week the people of Haverhill were invited down to Mr. Tyler's to pick pigeons. Those who went had the meat of all they picked, and the Tylers had the feathers; and they made, says Jonathan Tyler, "four very decent beds of those feathers." The bodies of those pigeons, when dressed, dried, and preserved for the winter, were very palatable and nutritrious, and proved a good substitute for other meats, of which the inhabitants had been despoiled by the Huns and Goths of the north. And we are bound to recognize the Divine Goodness in this providential supply, when the ordinary means of subsistence were cut off. It generally characterizes the Divine Government, when He has tried his people.

I have already stated that the first settlers at Coos,

a number of them, at least, pitched their tents upon the meadows, with a view of making their permanent residence there, but were driven off by a flood in 1771. Mr. Wallace, of Thetford, has furnished me with some particulars relative to that freshet. He says, this was a destructive flood to many of the settlers. Some of their fields were buried in sand to the depth of two and three feet, and they not only lost more or less of their crops for that year, but their *soil* for a number of years. Some of their habitations were invaded and taken possession of by the water. Wallace went to the relief of a family in Bradford, who lived on the place now owned by Mr. Hunkins. It was the family of Hugh Miller. His wife was the sister of the far-famed Robert Rogers, the hero of St. Francois. When Wallace reached this habitation, he rowed his canoe into the house as far as the width of the house would receive it, took the family from the bed whereon they stood, and bore them to a place of safety. But Mrs. Miller, the next day seeing their few sheep standing on a small eminence on the meadow, surrounded by water, her husband being absent, resolved on rescuing them from their perilous situation. She pressed into her service a young man by the name of George Binfield, and they took a canoe, and set sail for the sheep. They reached the place, caught the sheep, tied their legs, placed them on board, and set out on their return voyage to the high lands; but when they came into a strong current, they were carried down stream, until the canoe struck a pine stub, and was capsized. All were precipitated into the water of the depth of ten feet. When our heroine arose, and her companion in adventures, they caught hold of a stub standing about five feet out of the water, and maintained their grasp until another boat was obtained, and they were liberated from their perilous situation; but the wrecked canoe and sheep were never heard from more. From this time, the people sought a more elevated situation for their habitations.

Jonathan Tyler, of Piermont, related an extraordinary fact which occurred in this great freshet. He said, a horse was tied to a log in a stack-yard, upon the great Ox Bow, in Newbury, and when the water arose, it took away the horse and the log to which he was made fast, and the horse was taken out of the river in Hanover alive, but soon died upon reaching the shore. He would, doubtless, have perished soon after breaking from his moorings in Newbury; but the log to which he was tied kept his head above water, and prolonged his life many hours. Col. Howard told me, that in this same freshet some swine were taken away by the water in the north part of Haverhill, and were carried down to the Ox Bow, where they made good their standing upon the top of a hay-stack, where they remained capering about until the waters subsided, and the owners procured their property again. This calamity was not of equal extent with that of the Northern Army; but it was so intimately connected with it, it was severely felt, and it seemed as though God had a controversy with these people.

We may learn something of the facilities for travelling south and east from Haverhill Corner, so late as 1771, by the following facts. Jonathan Tyler came into Piermont in the autumn of 1768, and he says, "They seldom attempted to ride on horseback to Haverhill for several years after they came to Coos, owing to the badness of the road;" and I have heard it said by Judge Ladd and others, that a man from Charlestown came to Haverhill, and mired his horse so deeply on Haverhill Common, near Towle's tavern, that was, that he had to procure assistance to extricate the animal; and the horse was rendered so lame as to be unable to proceed on the journey for some days.

About this time, Col. Charles Johnston and several others had been to Plymouth, and thought they would return by Tarleton's Pond. They were retarded by the roughness of the travelling, beyond their expectations, and they were overtaken by nightfall. They made their way for a time by *feeling* of the trees to see if they were *spotted;* but they at length could feel no *spots,* and despaired of finding a settlement, or camp, that night; and making a virtue of necessity, they resolved to stand upon their posts like good soldiers, and wait for the return of day. It was a long night; but day at length dawned upon them, and, to their surprise and joy, they found themselves posted near the little brook, east of the establishment of Andrew Martin, one hundred and fifty rods, perhaps, east of the colonel's own habitation! For this reason, and because, I think, the brook is yet nameless, I would call it *Happy Brook,* we and our children, *forever!*

In the autumn of 1772, John McConnell and family left Pembroke, N. H., for the Coos, and when they came upon Baker's River, the intelligence reached Haverhill that they were advancing. Upon this, Jonathan McConnel, brother of John, went forth on horseback to meet them, and to render them assistance. The next morning early, Richard Wallace left Col. Johnston's on horseback, to go out and render them still further aid, taking in a freight of provisions. Jonathan McConnell met the family sixteen miles from Haverhill, took one of the children and some baggage, and set out for Haverhill. Wallace met Jonathan returning near the height of land, and he promised to stop at the camp near Eastman's Brook, and wait until Wallace and the family should come up, and all spend the night together. Wallace proceeded on, and met the family near night. They were in a miserable plight. They were all on foot, without shoes or stockings, and an old beast, a mere apology for a horse, staggering under the weight of a few necessary articles for the family; some scolding, some crying, and some laughing. It was soon agreed that Wallace should take two of the children, one a huge girl of twelve years, and another of two years, (which would have been the infant, had there not been another younger,) and return to Eastman's Brook, and the rest of the family was to reach there, if possible.

But in carrying this resolve into effect, Wallace met with an unexpected embarrassment. It would be impossible for the girl of twelve to hold on, in passing the sloughs and over logs, to ride in the usual manner of females. But as Wallace was at his wit's end to know how to arrange matters to his mind, the mother stepped forward, and, by a single

flash of her genius, cut the Gordian knot. "In
fa'th," said she, "there must be a leg on each side o'
the horse." And so the girl came into Haverhill.

But as Wallace ascended the height of land, he
became pretty well convinced that the family could
not make Eastman's Brook that night, and as there
was a camp on the height of land, which they must
pass, he dismounted, took a loaf of bread, run a pole
through it, and raised it above the top of the camp
outside, for the double purpose of keeping it from
the wolves, and of exhibiting to the family; but, by
some fatality, they did not see it, and passed on; but
as they did not reach the camp at Eastman's Brook,
they laid out all night, without food or covering.

Wallace had a hard task of it, likewise; for when
he came to the camp at Eastman's Brook, where
Jonathan McConnel proposed to stop, and to have a
fire for their comfort, he found no McConnel, no fire,
and not anything to make one of. McConnel had
concluded to make Haverhill that night, and leave
the rest to shift for themselves. Wallace now found
himself under the necessity of pursuing his journey
under circumstances "somewhat alarming, and very
disagreeable," as he said in a prior adventure. Beside this great lump of animated nature holding on
to him in the rear, he carried the child of two years

before him; and as the night drew on, it became drowsy, and sunk down into his arms very heavily. For a time, he kept it awake by calling its attention to the howling of the wolves in the vicinity; but at length nature was overpowered, and the child sunk down into a profound slumber, and he bore it into the Corner in this condition. They arrived at Col. Charles' house at twelve at night, a full moon favoring them. The colonel was up, and had a good fire, some expecting them, from what Jonathan McConnel had told him. But Wallace was so much exhausted by fatigue, and benumbed by the cold, that he fainted on coming to the fire. The family arrived the next day, and in just six months from that time the girl whom Wallace brought in, was married to Jonathan Tyler, of Piermont, at the age of *twelve years and six months.* The Rev. Peter Powers married them. This was the first marriage in *Piermont.*

At the time when these events, already stated, occurred, and for some years afterwards, it was not the expectation of the people at Coos that they should ever have a road through to Plymouth for loaded teams, but their hopes rested on Charleston for heavy articles; and the first time an ox-team went through, it was effected by a company, who went out expressly for the purpose, with Jonathan

McConnel at their head. It was an expedition that excited much interest with the inhabitants at home, and the progress of the adventurers was inquired for from day to day; and when they were making Haverhill Corner upon their return, the men went out to meet and congratulate them; and, as they came in, the cattle were taken possession of in due form, and conducted to sweet-flowing fountains and well-stuffed cribs for the night. Their masters were served in the style of lords, and their narrations of the feats of "Old Broad" at the sloughs, the patient endurance of "Old Berry" at the heights, and the stiff hold-back of "Old Duke" at the narrows, were listened to by their owners, with the liveliest demonstrations of joy.

What feeble impressions do the children and grandchildren of those early adventurers have of the difficulties which their ancestors surmounted to put their descendants into their present inheritance! Nor is the change greater in the face of the country, and in the condition of the roads, than it is in many other things. Contemplate the then state of schools. Mr. Wallace, to whom I am indebted for so many facts in respect to the first settlers, writes, that when he came to Haverhill, in 1769, at the age of sixteen, he did not know his alphabet, could not write his name, and his first attempt at writing was upon birch bark, with a *turkey's* quill. He further thinks that in 1772, not more than one school could be found in every ten miles, on either side of the river, from Orford to the Upper Coos. These were generally constituted by a few neighbors combining and hiring an instructor for a few weeks in the winter; their teachers being very inadequate, and their only books the Psalter and Primer. Compare these means with those now enjoyed by the rising generation; and let those who have made themselves merry by reciting the grammatical errors and orthographical blunders of their ancestors, perform a more splendid part in the great drama of human life; or let them ingenuously confess that they are debtors to those who received little, but did much, and left an example worthy of imitation by all their descendants; for it is to be had in lasting remembrance, that by these men, thus educated, our freedom was obtained, and those institutions founded, which are our blessing and our boast, and are the admiration of the world.

Speaking of the first settlers, Mr. Wallace further says, "Those who first settled Haverhill and Newbury were, for the most part, men of some property, and were able to furnish themselves with land, some stock, and tools, to hire laborers, and, in a short time, their houses were well furnished, *for that day.* They were laborious, prudent, and economical, but were very kind to the poor and sick. They were strict in their religious principles, and all attended religious worship on the Sabbath, neither men nor women esteeming it a hard service to travel on foot, four or six miles, with children in their arms, to hear the gospel."

Another class of persons, he mentions, that were in more indigent circumstances. They labored hard in the house and in the field, and whose earthly fare was coarse, and sometimes scanty. Their beds consisted principally of straw, and it was no uncommon thing for families to lie on the floor, and some on the ground, before the fire. Their bowls, dishes and plates were all of wood, although in a few families, a little pewter was seen. This class of persons, he relates, more generally settled in Piermont and Bradford, although there were families there in more eligible circumstances. The style of living in all the settlements was similar where they possessed the means. Boiled meat, peas or beans, and potatoes, formed their repast at noon; at night and morning, pea or bean broth, and sometimes milk porridge; "but," says Mr. Wallace, "we never thought of having meat more than once a day, and I never drank a cup of tea during the three years and a half that I lived at Coos." Many wore Indian stockings and moccasins of *raw hide*, when tanned leather could not be obtained ; and some of the wealthier had Indian blankets cut into box coats, and wore *buff caps*. Their clothing, in general, consisted of linen.

I will now leave the settlements at Coos for a time. in their peaceful and thriving situation, and proceed to give a concise history of some of the settlements in towns south of them, which brought neighbors to Haverhill and Newbury, and opened the wilderness between them and Charlestown. For seven years subsequent to the settlement of Coos, there was no inhabitant in the town of Piermont. But in the spring of 1768, Ebenezer White, Levi Root, and Daniel Tyler, came into the town, and settled on the meadows. In the autumn of that year, David Tyler, wife, and son Jonathan came on from Lebanon, in Connecticut. This is that Jonathan Tyler, who married Sarah McConnel, as already related. Tyler relates that wild game was exceedingly abundant in Piermont in the winter of 1769. Moose yarded upon the meadows that winter. Bears, wolves, and deer were ever present, and some of them quite officious. Several years after David and Jonathan Tyler came into the town, a bear came into their barn-yard at different times, "while men slept," and destroyed their sheep. This was sport for Bruin, but death to the Tylers. At length, Jonathan Tyler was aroused to a just sense of the injury and indignity inflicted upon them, and he resolved on revenge. He procured three guns, and charged them heavily with powder and ball, and retained them as "minute men," for any emergency. A few nights after this array of defence, Tyler heard the cry of distress in his yard. He sprang from his bed, threw on some light article of dress, seized his guns, and sallied forth, breathing slaughter and death. As soon as he came near the yard, he saw his bearship devouring his prey beneath his feet. Without preamble or apology, the three guns were "let off" in rapid succession, and every ball took effect. One penetrated the heart, and the assassin fell dead upon his prey, a huge enemy to the fleecy fold.

At this time, Tyler says, they went to Gen. Morey's mill at Orford, for grinding, which mill stood near where Capt. Daton's mill now stands. He had been to Charlestown for seed corn; and to Northfield, Mass., in a canoe, for bread-stuffs. But this must have been when the crops were cut off at Coos.

At one period of this settlement, the greater portion of the inhabitants bore some one of the following

6

catalogue of names:—Root, Crook, Cox, Stone, Daley, Bailey. They employed Dr. Samuel Hale, of Orford, for their physician. He was a high free-liver, and a facetious character, and used to amuse himself by speaking of his patrons in Piermont in the following couplet:—

"The Roots, and Crooks, and Elijah Daley,
Coxes and Stones, and Solomon Bailey."

But the merry doctor had to bear the expense of his own amusement; for when these families came to learn the use he made of their names, they took it in high dudgeon, and would never afterward employ him as their physician.

Jonathan Tyler, of whom I have spoken repeatedly, served his country in the time of the revolutionary war, and when our troops retreated from Ticonderoga, at the approach of Burgoyne's army, he was taken captive, but did not remain long in captivity. The manner of his escape was on this wise:—He was held as a prisoner of war for a time on the west side of Lake George, now called Lake Horican. For a time, he and two or three others of his fellow-prisoners were kept in "durance vile," and were watched with the utmost vigilance; but as they manifested no uneasiness themselves in their novel circumstances, their masters began to relax their vigilance, and they were permitted to go among the British troops, and to labor with them. At length, the British determined on building a block-house on the east side of the lake, and Jonathan Tyler, Daniel Bean, and another by the name of Cowdry, volunteered to go and help build it. After laboring a day or two, their axes needed grinding, and they were permitted to go to a spring of water just over a rise of ground, to bring water for grinding, and for other uses of the company. A bark had been laid down into the fountain, which conducted the water off, and rendered it very convenient in taking water at the lower end of the spout. Tyler hung his pail on the end of the spout, and while it was filling, he, Bean, and Cowdry, concluded to take *French leave*, and did so; and Tyler says, "He don't know but his pail hangs there yet." But the poor fellows had like to have perished with hunger. They left without a particle of food, and without arms and ammunition, and the first four days after their elopement, while they were hid in the woods west of the Hudson River, they had nothing to satisfy the cravings of hunger but leaves, buds and twigs of trees, and the roots which they dug out of the ground. And between the Hudson and the Connecticut, they sustained a like fast; but when they came to settlements in the Connecticut Valley, they were the happiest of mortals, and concluded they had done their part towards the achievement of our independence. David Tyler and wife, the parents of Jonathan Tyler, both lived to a great age. They attained to nearly ninety-five years.

The Congregational church was constituted in this town in 1771. The Rev. John Richards was settled as their pastor in 1776, and labored with them twenty-six years, and took a dismissal in 1802. The Rev. Jonathan Hovey was settled over them in 1810, and continued his labors five years. Rev. Robert Blake commenced his labors among them in 1819, and continued them, with some interruptions, until 1836. The statement in the Gazetteer of New Hampshire, that the first settlement in Piermont was in 1770, is an error.

ORFORD.

The town of Orford, which is ten miles south of Haverhill, and seventeen north of Hanover, was first settled in 1765. Daniel Cross and wife were the first who came into the place, from Lebanon, Ct. They came in June of this year, and pitched their tent near where the Sawyers afterward settled, upon the river road, south of Orford village. John Mann, Esq., and wife, whose maiden name Lydia Porter, both of Hebron, Conn., came into Orford in the autumn of 1765. Mann was twenty-one years of age, his wife seventeen years and six months. They left Hebron on the 16th of October, and arrived in Orford on the 24th of the same month. They both mounted the same horse, according to Puritan custom, and rode to Charlestown, N. H., nearly one hundred and fifty miles. Here Mann purchased a bushel of oats for his horse, and some bread and cheese for himself and wife, and set forward—Mann on foot; wife, oats, bread and cheese, and some clothing, on horseback.

From Charlestown to Orford there was no road but a horse-track, and this was frequently hedged across by fallen trees; and when they came to such an obstruction, which could not be passed round, Mann, who was of a gigantic stature, would step up, take the young bride, and set her upon the ground; then the oats, bread and cheese; and, lastly, the old mare was made to leap the windfall; when all was reshipped, and the voyage was resumed. This was acted over, time and again, until the old beast became impatient of delay, and coming to a similar obstruction, while Mann was some rods in the rear, she pressed forward, and leaped the trunk of a large tree, resisting all the force her young rider could exert; and when Mann came up, which he did in a trice, *there* lay the bride upon the ground, with all the baggage resting upon her. The old creature, however, had the civility not to desert them in this predicament, and as no bones were broken, and no joints dislocated, they soon resumed their journey; Mann, for the rest of the way, constituted the van instead of the rear guard.

When they arrived in Orford, they very naturally made Daniel Cross' tent their first resting place. They were received with all that cordiality and hospitality which characterize those who are separated from all friends, and are enclosed by the solitudes of a vast wilderness. Cross had reared a shelter for his cow adjoining his own tent, and for that night the cow was ejected, and Cross and his wife occupied her apartment, while Mann and his wife improved the parlor. But they were doomed to a sad adventure that night. Cross had felled a large tree, the butt end of which constituted no inconsiderable portion of one side of his house. Into this log he had bored two holes, about four feet apart, and sharpening two sapling poles, he had driven them horizontally into the log, to form the two side pieces of a bedstead. The other end of the poles were supported by two perpendicular posts, in the manner of ordinary bedsteads. Elm bark served for cord and sacking. This rigging was adequate to sustain Cross and his companion, a light couple; but when Mann and his partner came into possession, it was another affair. Mann was of gigantic stature. Soon after all had retired to rest, this frail fabric of a bedstead suddenly gave way with a loud crash, which frightened the tenants of both apartments prodigiously. Mrs. Mann screamed, and this was suddenly responded to from Cross' apartment, "What *is* the matter?" But after mutual explanations and apologies, Mann and his wife resumed a recumbent position upon the *floor*, and enjoyed a refreshing sleep, with the exception of an occasional interruption from a sudden burst of laughter in the cow apartment, where Cross and his wife lay, reflecting upon the startling scene through which they had passed unscathed. Esquire Mann related this adventure after he was more than eighty years of age, and he did it with that impassioned emotion, which tended to impress the mind of the hearer as though it was an event that had recently transpired.

Soon after Mann came to Orford, he took a log-canoe near where Cross lived, and ascended the river to the place where the Orford bridge now is. He went ashore to reconnoitre and to spy out the land. The soil supported a huge growth of wood and a dense underbrush. The surface was covered with a tall, thick, and white moss, and had every appearance of being boggy. Mann thought he would penetrate a little way into the forest, and take some care and not needlessly wet his feet. He accordingly stepped with caution, jumped from one little mound to another, and when he got upon a windfall, he would improve the whole length of it. But while thus making his way, he lost the centre of gravity, when on an old log, and fell to the ground. But instead of plunging into a bog, as he expected, he came " plump on to hard and dry soil," that beautiful bottom land which he and others have so long cultivated to great advantage.

Mrs. Mann, after they were settled in their own tent, went to the river, and brought all the water they used in a three-pint basin, with the exception of washing days.

John Mann, Jun., Esq., was the first English child born in the town, May 21, 1766, and if now living, must be in his seventy-fourth year. The same autumn in which Mann came into Orford, Jonathan and Edward Sawyer, Gen. Israel Morey, and a Mr. Caswell, all from Connecticut, came in and settled.

The first church in Orford was constituted in 1770. The Rev. Oliver Noble, their first minister, was ordained, November 5, 1771, and was dismissed, December 31, 1777. Then there was an interregnum of about ten years, and the Rev. John Sawyer was ordained over them, October 22, 1787. He continued with them but about eight years, and was dismissed 1795. Rev. Sylvester Dana was ordained over them, May 20, 1801. He continued their pastor twenty-one years—dismissed, April 30, 1822. Rev. James D. Farnsworth was ordained, January 1, 1823. Mr. Farnsworth has been dismissed, and he has a successor, Mr. Campbell; but the dates of those events I must leave to my successor in gathering statistics.

Mr. Mann relates that when he came into the town, and for some years after, deer and bear were very numerous, and some moose in the east part of the town. He has been up on the elevated ground, east of the river road, after a new-fallen snow, and seen deer tracks almost as plentifully imprinted as we see sheep tracks where the latter are yarded.

As Mann came on from Charlestown, he found in the town of Claremont, two openings by young men of the name of Dorchester. In Cornish there was but one family, that of Moses Chase. In Plainfield there was one family, Francis Smith. The wife was "terribly" home-sick, and she declared she "would not stay there in the woods." In Lebanon, there were three families, Charles Hill, son, and son-in-
6*

law, a Mr. Pinnick. In Hanover, there was one family, Col. Edmund Freeman, and several young men, who were making settlements. In Lyme, there were three families, all by the name of Sloan—John, William, and David. This statement differs materially from what we find in the Gazetteer of New Hampshire in respect to the first settlers in those towns. But I have long since lost all confidence in gazetteers, when they attempt to give facts anterior to *recorded* facts, and they never can be depended upon, so long as no better means are employed than those which have been used to gain information. The method has ordinarily been to write to some post-master, justice of the peace, or some other man, and request him to furnish them with the early settlement of the town, both recorded facts and traditionary tales. But where is there a man, who, upon such an application, will devote one week to the examination of records, or to visit the aged to gain information? Not one, we believe, in fifty, if there is one in a hundred. And in most cases, it would require all of one month to make a correct report. In general, there is not one line on record in regard to first settlers. Their records begin with the charter, which might have come into existence years before the settlement, or years afterward; but most persons are ready to take it for granted, that their town was settled the year it was chartered, and that some of the first names specified in the charter were the first settlers. But nothing can be more uncertain than this. Besides, every town has its favorite stories derived from tradition, which they wish to establish ; and almost every man wishes to bring forward his ancestors to figure as principal characters, which never were such, and it may be, never were distinguished for anything, unless it were stupidity or knavery. But this application furnishes him with an opportunity to palm upon the public a bloated account of his pedigree, and, instead of going to the ancient records, if there are any, or to the aged, he sits down and writes what is most satisfactory to himself, and it soon appears as matter of history. I need not specify particular instances of this fraud. They are many. Almost every town, if they should make a thorough investigation, will find that they have been misrepresented, and in some instances grossly insulted. I invite the attention of the people of Haverhill, especially, to these remarks. I would not diminish the interest which the public may feel in Farmer and Moore's Gazetteer of New Hampshire. They have done well. Every family ought to possess it. It is worth a million of Thompson's Gazetteer of Vermont ; but they ought to have sent a competent agent into every town in the state to collect statistics, before they had published. Lebanon is made the first town settled north of Charlestown, before Haverhill or Newbury, contrary to the united testimony of the first settlers in all the towns above them. Esquire Mann and Esquire Otis Freeman agree in their statement in respect to Lebanon. Has Lebanon authentic documents to show that their town was settled as early as 1760, or the spring of 1761? They can show that their town was *chartered* then; but can they show that it was *settled?* If they can, let the truth stand. Plainfield, Mann and Freeman tell us, had one family in it in 1765; our Gazetteer shows us two men there, L. Nash and J. Russell, in 1764, and the next year, when Mann and Freeman came through, 1765, it tells us of a church organized, and a settled minister, Rev. Abraham Carpenter. Has the town these documents? If they have, it is the first instance in which I have found the first settlers deviating from the truth; but they harmonize with wonderful exactness when we compare all their statements.

I have nothing further to speak of Lyme, that is prior to what is recorded and published. The church, according to the Gazetteer, was constituted in 1772. Rev. William Conant was settled as their pastor in 1773. Rev. Nathaniel Lambert, previously settled at Newbury, Vt., was settled in Lyme in 1811. Rev. Baxter Perry was settled, 1821. The Rev. Erdix Tenney is their present pastor.

The first family which came into Hanover was that of Col. Edmund Freeman, who lived in the east part of the town. He came in May, 1765, from Mansfield, Conn. He brought with him a wife and two children, and his brother, Otis Freeman, then of the age of seventeen. Several other young men came in the same season. Deacon Jonathan Curtis and son came; but he did not move his family until 1766. Col. Edmund Freeman gave the name of Hanover to the town.

I have already related the circumstances of the first marriage in the town. The first death which occurred was that of a child in the family of Deacon Benton; it died of consumption at the age of fourteen months. The first meeting-house was built of logs, and stood near the river, between Timothy Smith's and Mr. Tisdale's. The proprietors of the town first employed the Rev. Knight Saxton, of Colchester, Conn., to preach to these settlers in the summers of 1766 and 1767. Subsequently, Dr. McClure, of Boston, was employed to preach to the people; and Eden Burroughs, D. D., of Stratford,

Conn., who had been previously settled at Killingly, Windham Co., Conn., was installed over this church and people in 1772. Dr. Burroughs was dismissed in 1809, and Rev. Josiah Towne was ordained, June, 1814. Mr. Towne has been dismissed, and another clergyman has been settled; but I know not his name.

A full and satisfactory account of the origin of Dartmouth College, in the town of Hanover, of its progress and prosperity, has been given to the public through different channels, and is so far above my feeble praise, it needs not to be further noticed in these sketches.

I now pass on to the west side of the river, and speak of the settlement of Norwich, Vt. I shall relate a plain story, which I took from the lips of Rev. Asa Burton, D. D., of Thetford, Vt., when he was at the age of 72, and sound, both in mind and body. He relates that his father, Jacob Burton, of Stonington, Conn., came to Norwich first in the summer of 1764, and viewed the country for the purpose of locating himself, provided he was suited with appearances. "At that time," he says, "there was no inhabitant in the town." The next year, 1765, his father returned to Norwich, and laid out a part of the town into lots; and in June, 1776, he came with

Asa, his son, then in his fourteenth year, and some other hands, and built a saw-mill, a little west of Norwich Plain. Dr. Burton says, "There were then but two families in the town; one by the name of Messenger, who lived at the west end of the present bridge leading from Hanover to Norwich; and a Mr. Hutchinson, who lived near where the Military Academy now stands. Hanover Plain was at this time a thick pine forest." Messenger and Hutchinson came into Norwich either in 1765, or the spring of 1766. He further says, "There was no minister, at that time, nearer than Newbury and Haverhill, at Coos; but in a few years Mr. Conant settled at Lyme, Dr. Burroughs at Hanover, Mr. Isaiah Potter at Lebanon, and Mr. Lyman Potter at Norwich." Where, now, is Rev. Mr. Carpenter of Plainfield, in 1765, at the distance of twelve or fourteen miles from Norwich?

But now for Thompson's Gazetteer of Vermont, published at Montpelier, in 1824. He has it, that in 1763, Jacob Fenton, Ebenezer Smith, and John Slafter, came into Norwich from Mansfield, Conn.; that at this time there were two men settled in Hanover; that in July, Smith and Slafter left Fenton on Wednesday, for the purpose of hoeing corn in Lebanon, and that on their return on Saturday, at evening, they found Fenton dead in their camp. It appeared afterwards, that a Mr. Freeman, of Hanover, happened over at Norwich, and found Fenton sick, tarried with him until he died, and then went to Lebanon to procure help to bury him, and he was buried, July 15, 1765; that there were four families moved into Norwich in 1764, and from that time the settlement advanced rapidly. Now, for the correctness of this statement. He says, that in 1763, there were two men in Hanover, and one of them, at least, was a Mr. Freeman. But the very Mr. Freeman here alluded to, which was Col. Otis Freeman, gave me the particulars of his finding Fenton sick in his tent—he had had a fit; and that it was the same year he and his brother came into Hanover, viz., 1785. Thompson further states, that Fenton was taken sick, and died in July, 1763, and was buried July 15, 1765. According to this, there were but three years which intervened between his death and burial! But this might be owing to his sudden death, and the extreme warmth of the season. Again, four families moved into Norwich in 1764, and from this period the settlement advanced with *considerable rapidity.* But in 1765, when they concluded to bury Fenton, they had to depend on Freeman, of Hanover, to go after Smith and Slafter to

Lebanon, to procure help for the burial, and Fenton is left "alone" in the town! Now, let us take this which way we will, it is nothing but jargon; and it shows conclusively that there was not one moment given to the examination of dates by the compiler of this work, but whatever was sent to him in the form of a statistic, was received as authentic.

I notice these egregious blunders to confirm what I have already said, that gazetteers cannot be relied upon for statements which are not supported by written documents. And I have another object in view, which is, to show those who would be compilers of gazetteers, that they have something to do besides calling for crude papers, and publishing them. No man ought to think of publishing another gazetteer, either of New Hampshire or Vermont, in a less compass than nine hundred pages of large octavo, first expending three thousand dollars in collecting and arranging materials, and then giving it to the public at three dollars per copy.

There is but one apparent discrepancy between Dr. Burton's statement, and Col. Otis Freeman's. I say *apparent*, because it can be easily reconciled. Dr. Burton says there were but two families in the town when he came in 1766; whilst Freeman says, Smith and Slafter were there in 1765, and the families mentioned by Burton bore the name, Messenger and Hutchinson. But suppose Smith and Slafter were there in 1766, Burton was not speaking of single men, but of men with families. I find the first settlers made this distinction in all their statements. Again, nothing was more common than for young men to come in, and labor one season, and then retire, and we never hear of them again : they have sold out to another; or they were in the service of another man. Smith and Slafter might have been in Norwich in 1765, and not in 1776, but there again in 1767. But we must keep in mind that Mr. Jacob Burton, father of Asa, said there was no one in the town in 1764.

I again take up the thread of history. Asa Burton continued to labor for his father until he was twenty-one years of age, at which time he entered upon his studies preparatory for college, under the tuition of Mr. John Smith, subsequently the professor of the learned languages in Dartmouth College, and he entered college in a little more than one year from the commencement of his studies.

There was one adventure of young Burton, at the age of eighteen years, which deserves a place in these sketches, and which cannot fail to call the attention of the people of Norwich to times gone by. A large female bear had followed a cow belonging to Jacob Burton, until they both came near the house; when the bear was discovered by one of the sons of Jacob Burton, and was driven off from the cow on to a ledge of rocks, north of Norwich Plain, and east of the road which runs north and south. But the young man was not content with releasing the cow from danger, but he determined to worry the bear; and as he saw she was clambering up the rocks to pass over the ledge, he ran round, and gained the top of the ledge first; and here he hallooed Asa, who was chopping on the plain south of them. As soon as Asa heard the call, he ran at the top of his speed with his axe to the scene of action. By this time, the bear had ascended to the verge of the rocks, where Asa's brother stood, and she seemed inclined to contest for a prior claim she had to a passage that way. Asa saw the predicament of his brother, and fearing he should lose his game, if the bear made good her standing on the top of the precipice, he pressed up the rocks in the rear of the bear with all the haste he could possibly make. This inspired his brother aloft with fresh resolution to keep the bear from gaining the top, and with kicks and thrusts he succeeded in keeping her below the precipice. And so sharp was this contest, that the bear did not appear to notice the approach of her assailant in the rear, until Asa drew upon her with the head of his axe, and laid the blow upon her rump, which knocked her down; and as he was unacquainted with the hardiness and strength of the bear, he supposed the victory was already achieved; but she soon found her legs again, and plied them with greater diligence than ever in making her escape. The bear now relinquished her hope of ascending the precipice, and commenced descending the hill in an oblique direction, with Asa pressing hard upon her rear. But in his endeavors to surmount some windfalls over which the bear had passed, he fell backwards upon the ground; at which moment the bear turned back, sprang upon the log, showed her terrific teeth, and appeared in the very attitude of leaping upon him. This was the first moment that taught young Burton his danger, and it brought him upon his feet with new inspiration, and he resolved that henceforth he would neither give or take quarter. He made at the bear with redoubled fury, and compelled her to retreat down the hill, and as she came near the base she became entangled among the logs, and here our young hero made a second onset, and fetched her to the ground; then turning the edge of the axe, he sunk it into her throat to the very bone, and the victory was his. This bear was one of the largest class, and gave tokens that she was then employed in rearing her young. My only remark in the conclusion is, that others may kill bears, and I will record their deeds.

The Rev. Lyman Potter was ordained over the church and congregation in Norwich, in 1775, and was dismissed, 1800. Rev. James Woodward was installed over this church and society, 1804. Previous to 1820, a new church and society was formed upon Norwich Plain, and the Rev. Rufus W. Bailey was settled over them in 1820, and was dismissed in 1824. Rev. James Woodward was dismissed from the north church, and the Rev. Samuel Goddard was installed their pastor, 1822. The Rev. Thomas Hall has been settled over the church and society upon the Plain, but is now dismissed from that charge.

Thetford was first settled, in 1764, by John Chamberlain, from Hebron, Conn. And in 1765, at the time when Esquire Mann came into Orford, there were two other families, one by the name of Baldwin, and the other by the name of Hosford. Chamberlain was very industrious, and somewhat parsimonious withal, and soon rose to a kind of independence of his neighbors, which *he,* as well as *they,* seemed to be fully conscious of. Chamberlain did not rise, however, above the reach of envy, and the wags of that day selected him for their butt, at which they aimed their pointed arrows of wit and sarcasm. It was not long before Chamberlain was furnished with a penultima to his gift name, as he seemed to feel that his parents had wronged him in infancy by deciding that he should bear the undignified appellation—*John*, it being only a monosyllable. He was, therefore, dubbed *Quail John*, for what reason I have never learned; but it adhered to him through life. And in proof of the fact that the Muses either preceded in their flight to this section of country the first settlers, or very soon followed their trail, I will put down some lines which were composed, and often repeated in the hearing of him whose praises they would celebrate:

"Old Quail John was the first that came on,
As poor as a calf in the spring;
But now he is rich as Governor Fitch,
And lives like a lord or a king."

Fitch, to whom reference is here made, was one of the governors of Connecticut about these days. But Chamberlain was destined to higher and less perishable honors than the simple elongation of his name. To him was born the first English child that was ever born in the town; his name was Samuel.

Thetford did not settle a minister until the summer of 1773, when a man by the name of Clement Sumner was installed their pastor. We know not the place of his nativity. He graduated at Yale College in 1758, settled in Keene, N. H., June 11, 1761, and was dismissed, April 30, 1772. He remained in Thetford but little more than two years. He became a tory, left them without asking for a dismission, and went to Swanzey, N. H., where he became a Universalist preacher, and continued in that persuasion until his death. He was the source of much trouble to the town of Thetford. He took from them a fine right of land which fell to him by settlement, and divided the church and town. Wallace says, "He was no more fit to preach than a fox is to make a gold watch." We do not learn that there was ever any lack of fellowship between him and his Universalist brethren at Swanzey.

Wallace settled in the west part of Thetford, six miles from the river, where he lived to an advanced period of life. He relates a distressing scene which was occasioned by an alarm that was spread through the country in the summer of 1777. Wallace was at Charlestown, N. H., when an American scouting party came in with a British scouting party, as prisoners of war, from Burgoyne's army. Upon these prisoners were found papers, purporting that three detachments of British soldiers and tories were to be sent out to the Connecticut valley—one to Newbury, one to Royalton, and one to Charlestown, N. H. This was nothing but a strategem of Burgoyne's to divert the Americans from his army, and the scout was sent out for the purpose of being taken with these papers on their hands, and it succeeded wonderfully. The news spread through the country like electricity.

Wallace made all speed for Thetford, and found on his arrival that the people had gained the intelligence that they were to be invaded by the enemy, and they were pressing in for the river from Strafford and other settlements, in the utmost consternation. This was done by order of the Committee of Safety. Strafford was literally emptied. There were a number of tories in that town. There were eight brothers in one family went over to the British at once, and they carried some others with them; and their property was all taken and sold for public use. Those who remained true to their country's cause expected to feel the vengeance of these enemies; and when Wallace came home, he met, between the place where Thetford meeting-house now stands and his habitation, men, women and children, who had forsaken houses and lands, and everything which they could not conveniently carry; some in carts, some on sleds, some in sleighs, in mid-summer, and some on foot. They had their hands full of light articles of clothing, and packs stuffed upon their backs, and were driving before them cattle, horses, sheep, and swine. The mixed noise of these different kinds of animals, and the cries of women and children, who expected to be overtaken every minute, murdered and scalped by the infuriated Indians, tories, and British, were enough to affect the stoutest heart. Wallace was looking out for his wife, whom he supposed to be in the caravan; but they all passed him, and he saw nothing of his beloved Creusa. Several times he was confident that bright image appeared to his view in the motley throng; but, as they advanced, behold! it was another, and not she—

"—— tenuesque recessit in auras."

Wallace now put spurs to his steed, that he might the sooner dissolve the doubts which had arisen in his own breast, allay the anxiety he felt for his better *self*. When he arrived at his hut, he found his wife sticking by the stuff. Having no horse or oxen to aid her in transporting the goods to the river, she had resolved to wait and see if there was cause for all this trepidation and flight. She had, however, commenced carrying their household stuff into the woods, and covering it with bushes, that it might not fall into the hands of the invaders, should they suddenly appear. They both completed the work which his wife had so heroically commenced, and then both mounted their horse, and rode for the settlements at the river. The next day, Wallace and another took a team, and went and brought in the goods; and as soon as they were disposed of, Wallace enlisted to go in pursuit of Burgoyne and his army, wisely concluding it best so to press the lion in his den, that his whelps should not feel at liberty to go abroad and devastate the surrounding country. And this was the effect of Burgoyne's stratagem generally. It returned upon his own head. After the surrender of Burgoyne and his army, October 17, 1777, Wallace returned to his hut in December, where he and his wife lived through the succeeding winter, without any chimney, hearth, or floor, except three or four loose boards to set their pole bedstead upon, that was corded with elm bark.

Mrs. Wallace deserves distinct notice in this place. At the time of the alarm, Wallace had corn, oats, and potatoes growing on his newly-cleared land. After he had gone in pursuit of Burgoyne, and the alarm had somewhat subsided, Mrs. Wallace travelled out six miles to see to their crops. She found the oats ripe for harvesting, and many of them lodged. She was all alone, and no man could be procured to assist her in gathering them, for all that could be spared had gone to the field of battle. Nothing daunted at this, she took a scythe and mowed them, dried them, raked them into bunches, bound them, and stacked them in good style. She then took an axe, cut poles, fenced them about, and then went back to the river. When her corn-stalks were ripe for cutting, she went out, cut them, bound them, and put them on the top of her stack of oats. In like manner she went out and gathered the corn, and dug her potatoes, and secured both. She then went to work at clearing some ground which had been felled, and was burnt over the year before; and when her husband returned from the army, she had cleared and sown one acre of wheat; and during the absence of her husband she had travelled, in going to and from the river, seventy-two miles!

The following year they procured some sheep, which they had to yard in a pen near the house every night, to preserve them from the wolves, which were numerous. Wallace being at work at the river on a certain time, Mrs. Wallace could not find her sheep to yard them at evening, and as soon as it came on dark, the wolves set up a frightful howling, as it seemed, within twenty rods of the house. What to do for the safety of her sheep, she did not know; but on examination she found the gun was loaded ; she at once sallied forth and discharged the gun, to inform the wolves that something was there besides mutton. At twelve at night, she reloaded, and went forth and discharged her piece a second time. And before daylight, they heard from her the *third* time ; and at sunrise, she went out and found all her sheep near the pen, safe and sound, and the wolfish gentry swift on the retreat.

This woman became the mother of eleven children, nine of whom lived to enter into the married state, and to have families. In 1828, these parents had fifty grandchildren, and five great-grandchildren.

But the best part remains to be told. This woman served as an accoucheuse forty-five years, rode in seven towns, was present at the birth of twenty-one pair of twins, and one thousand, six hundred and twenty-four single births ; making, in all, one thousand, six hundred and sixty-six, and never lost a mother of whom she had the care.

Gentlemen and ladies of 1840, sitting in your broadcloth, silks and satins, what say you to these things ? Could not some things be done without steam, railroad, or piano forte ? I would leave you to pleasant reflections. Fidelity in a historian is a jewel.

There is one adventure of Wallace which must be recorded before we take leave of him. It took place in the fall of 1777, a little time before he returned to Thetford from the pursuit of Burgoyne, as I have already stated. I receive the facts in this case from two sources, viz, from David Johnson, Esq., of Newbury, Vt., to whom Wallace and Webster both related the story, and from the Hon. Simeon Short, Esq., of Thetford, who was Wallace's agent in procuring a pension, and who had, in behalf of Wallace, transmitted the following particulars to the Pension Office at Washington.

It will be recollected by those who are acquainted with the history of the war of the revolution, that as soon as the battle was fought at Bennington, and the Americans began to hope that Burgoyne's army would fall into their hands, they set about retaking the forts of Ticonderoga and Mount Independence, on the shores of Lake Champlain, which forts Burgoyne had left in his rear, supplied with troops for their defence. Ticonderoga was taken, and Mount Independence was straitly besieged for some time. There was a good deal of hard fighting, and it was confidently looked for, that Mount Independence would surrender; but they did not. The British shipping had full possession of the lake. Ticonderoga was upon the west side of the lake, and Mount Independence on the east side. Our troops on the west side could hold no communication with those who had invested Mount Independence, and of course they could have no concert in action. It was at this time, when the greatest solicitude was felt by the two American commanders to know each others' minds, that the following expedient was adopted by the commander at Ticonderoga. He called on his men to know if there were any two of them who would volunteer to swim the lake in the evening, and carry dispatches to Gen. Lincoln, near Mount Independence. For a time, none offered to undertake the hazardous enterprise; but when informed how much was probably depending upon it, Wallace of Thetford stepped forward, and said he would attempt it; and then followed him Ephraim Webster, of Newbury, who originated in New-Chester, N. H. The documents were made out and about sun-down, an officer took these two men on to an eminence which overlooked the lake, and he pointed out to them the course they must take to avoid discovery by the British shipping, and then about where they would probably find the American camp. At dusk of evening, the same officer attended them to the margin of the lake, assisted them to prepare for the voyage, and saw them set sail, little expecting, probably, ever to hear from them again ; for as they had to swim up and down the lake, in a zigzag course, to avoid the enemy, they must swim more than two miles before they could make terra firma, and it was so late in the season the water was quite cold. They rolled their dispatches in their clothes, and bound their clothes upon the back part of their neck, by cords passing round their foreheads and their clothes. As soon as they entered the water Wallace said to Webster, "We shall never reach shore, it is so cold ;" but this he said without any thought of relinquishing the enterprise. When about mid-way of the lake, the cords which fastened Wallace's clothes to his neck slipped down from his forehead to his throat, and it cut him so hard as almost to strangle him. He made several attempts to replace the string upon his forehead, but failed, and he was on the point of giving up all for lost. The thought, however, of the importance of his undertaking seemed to inspire him with new life and vigor, and he succeeded in replacing the string, and passed on without saying a word to dishearten Webster. They passed so near the British shipping as to hear the oft-repeated cry, "All's well !" They took no care to contradict that report, but buffeted the waves with stout hearts and sinewy limbs. They kept in company until they came near the eastern shore of the lake, when Webster seemed to fall into the rear, a few rods at the north of Wallace; and just as Wallace struck the twigs of a tree which lay extended into the lake, he heard Webster say, "Help, Wallace, I am drowning!" Wallace sprung to the shore, caught a stick, and rushed into the water, and extended it to Webster in the act of sinking, and drew him ashore. Webster could not stand; but Wallace rubbed him briskly, and got on his clothes, and he soon recovered so as to walk. How aptly the poet's description of Ulysses, when cast upon the coast of Phæacia, will apply to Webster, as drawn ashore by Wallace, the reader will judge:

> "From mouth and nose the briny torrent ran,
> And lost in lassitude, lay all the man;
> Deprived of voice, of motion, and of breath,
> The soul scarce waking in the arms of death."

Webster was so full of expressions of gratitude to Wallace for the preservation of his life, that Wallace had to caution him not to speak so loud, for the enemy would hear them.

But new difficulties now presented themselves. It was now dark, and they were in a strange place. The enemy was near, and had their sentinels on shore as well as the Americans. And, what was worst of all, they knew not the countersign of the Americans on that side of the lake. They started, however, in quest of the American camp, and after travelling about, nearly one hour, they were hailed by a British sentinel, and did but just make their escape. They then took a different direction, and Wallace gave both despatches into Webster's hands, and told him to keep in the rear, and he would go forward, and if he should happen to fall into the hands of the enemy, Webster might have opportunity to escape with the despatches. But they had not proceeded a great ways before Wallace was hailed by a sentinel—"Who comes there?" "A friend," says Wallace. "A friend to whom?" says the sentinel. "Advance and give the countersign." This was a fearful moment. Wallace hesitated for an instant, and then replied by way of question—"Whose friend are you?" The sentinel responded—"A friend to America!" "So am I," said Wallace, "and have important despatches for your general." They were immediately conducted to the general's quarters, the despatches were delivered, and Wallace and Webster were received with every mark of surprise and gratitude, and every thing was done to render them comfortable and happy. But Wallace never enjoyed the degree of health afterwards that he did prior to that chill and almost incredible effort. Wallace departed this life,

February 7, 1833, aged eighty. Mrs. Wallace died, May, 1831, aged eighty-one.

Webster's subsequent history is worthy of a passing notice. The last time he visited Newbury, he was residing among the Oneida Indians, New York. They had adopted him as their brother, promoted him to be chief in their tribe, and, to render the tie indissoluble, they had given him one of the black-haired maidens of the forest. Webster's health was not permanently injured by his dangerous adventure.

The church and people in Thetford remained in a divided state more than three years after Sumner left them, until Dr. Burton came among them, in 1778, at the age of twenty-seven years. He graduated at Dartmouth College in 1777, read divinity with Dr. Eleazer Wheelock, president of the college, until he was licensed to preach the gospel, and he then went and read with Dr. Hart, of Preston, New London Co., Conn. As soon as Dr. Burton came into Thetford, the unhappy divisions which had existed among them were all dissipated as by enchantment. They were all united in him, and all reconciled to each other. They gave him a unanimous call to settle with them in the gospel ministry, and he was ordained their pastor, January 19, 1779.

There were fifty-seven families in the town when

Dr. Burton settled among them. There were but two families then living west of the present meeting-house, viz, Richard Wallace, and a Mr. Osborn, living near Mr. Wallace. They had no meeting-house; and in the summer they held their meetings in a barn, and in a private dwelling in the winter. The first meeting-house was built of logs, and stood near the place where Dr. Solomon Heaton used to live, from half to three-fourths of a mile north-east of the present meeting-house, on the road leading from Thetford to East Fairlee and Orford. The seats in this meeting-house were movable forms, or benches, like those often found in school-houses for children to sit upon, and they were ranged on each side of the house, the ends pointing towards one broad aisle in the centre.

Dr. Burton related, in much good humor, one incident which occurred in that house, that was of a stirring quality. The doctor had a parishioner by the name of John Osman, and he was an abominable sleeper in the house of God. His habit in this was so inveterate as to resist all remonstrance. It so happened, on a very warm Sabbath in mid-summer, that Osman was seated on the end of one of those benches next to the aisle. He was facing the aisle, and, in order to find secure repose, he placed his elbows upon his knees, folded his arms, and leaned forward ; and in this position he fell into a profound slumber. The doctor saw him paying his devotions to Somnus, by now and then a significant nod and a reel of the body, but said nothing to disturb his repose. At length, Osman lost his balance, and pitched his whole length on to the floor, where he lay in the middle of the aisle, sprawled out like a spider ! The shock with the audience was electrical. Many sprang upon their feet, and some females shrieked out ; but when they saw Osman gathering up his limbs in the most deliberate manner, rubbing his eyes, and scratching his head, the transition from surprise to risibility was so sudden and powerful, that the impulse was irrepressible, and for a few moments the speaker himself labored to maintain the dignity and gravity of his station. But it proved a specific in Osman's case, for he was never known to sleep in meeting after that event. It might be well, perhaps, for some of our modern sleepers at the house of God, if they were to descend as low in the Valley of Humiliation as Osman did, provided their resurrection should be as triumphant.

At the settlement of the town of Thetford, and for a number of years subsequently to that period, bears, deer, and sables were numerous ; but we hear of no moose. Joel Strong, of Hebron, Conn., came into the town on the 7th of May, 1768, and found twelve families in the town. He first settled on the bottom lands of the Ompompanoosuc, and as soon as he began to raise corn, he was exceedingly annoyed by bears in his field, devouring his unripe corn. For a time he bore these injuries with all the meekness which necessity laid upon him ; but seeing increasing waste and destruction, he arose and shook himself, and resolved he would seek reprisal. And now the waxing moon smiled on his enterprise. He loaded his gun with two balls, took his powder-horn and bullet-pouch, and sallied forth to reconnoitre the position of his enemies. He had not proceeded far before he heard the ears of corn snap from their parent stalks, as though there were a husking with the Bruin gentry. Strong advanced slowly and cautiously until he secured a good shot, and then he "let off," and brought one huge fellow to the ground. This was a signal for others to retreat, and without looking to him whom he had disposed of, he pursued the flying foe as fast as his legs would carry him ; and two others ascended a large tree which stood near the border of the field. It was not sufficiently light for him to distinguish his game in the boughs, and he struck him up a fire at the foot of the tree, and there waited for the return of day. The returning sun showed him two sleek and lusty fellows, sitting in appropriate angles of the tree, formed by the union of large branches with the trunk. Strong now took deliberate aim at the heart, and down came his bearship from a goodly height, which made the ground tremble again. With all expedition he charged his gun the third time, and in a few moments the remaining bear joined his comrade upon the ground, and as they had been lovely in the eyes of each other in life, so they were not divided in their death. Strong was now at liberty to visit the one that was slain the night before, and he found them all bears of the first-class, which remunerated him for all previous losses, and their death secured his field from further depredations.

I have said Dr. Burton was ordained, January 19, 1779. The ministers called to ordain him were the following :—Rev. Messrs. Powers of Newbury, Conant of Lime, Burroughs of Hanover, Potter of Lebanon, and Potter of Norwich. The last-named gentlemen preached the sermon. But those who imposed hands, and he who received hands, have alike gone down to the dust. A new order of things has arisen ; and how forcibly are we impressed with the words of the apostle, *For what is your life? It is even a vapor, that appeareth for a little time, and then vanisheth away.*

But very few clergymen labored longer in their profession than Dr. Burton did; very few have been more successful in bringing sinners to salvation; and there are very few whose influence has been more extensively realized than his. He prepared more than a hundred young men for the ministry; and his Book of Essays, published in 1824, is rich in ideas, and although we may differ from him in our metaphysics, yet when men come to pay more regard to ideas than to their dress, and when they shall prefer *thinking* to light reading, Dr. Burton will be read with profit by every student in theology.

Dr. Burton departed this life, May 1, 1836, in the eighty-fourth year of his age, and in the fifty-seventh of his pastoral relation to the church and people of Thetford. " The memory of the just is blessed."

FAIRLEE.

Of Fairlee, East or West, I have little to say. In 1766, Mr. Baldwin, who is mentioned as one of the families settled in Thetford in 1765, moved from Thetford to East Fairlee, and commenced a settlement about half a mile south of the present meetinghouse, near where they turn off from the river road to go to Fairlee or Morey's Pond. Mr. Thompson in his Gazetteer dates the settlement of this town in 1768, and then he finds six men on the ground to begin the settlement. Esquire Mann, of Orford, says, Baldwin was his first neighbor west of him, and he is sure he came into Fairlee the year after Mann came to Orford. They both came from Hebron, Conn. Mann knew that Baldwin spent a year or so in Thetford, and then came up to Fairlee, and he tells us the very spot where he commenced. Mann could not mistake in this. I find that a new neighbor, in those days, was not looked upon as a trivial affair, and the time of its occurrence was retained with great accuracy. It may be there were six men in Fairlee in 1768 ; but Baldwin had been there two years previous.

BRADFORD.

Bradford was first settled in 1765, by a man by the name of John Osmer. He settled near the mouth of Wait's River, on the north bank, and I have been told there were traces of this settlement so late as 1824. This town was originally called Moretown ; but afterward it was changed to Bradford. This Osmer, or Hosmer, was a facetious character, and would make himself sport at the expense of others.

In 1765, soon after Hosmer moved into Bradford, there came to his hut a transient Irishman, and spent several days, laboring what he would for his board. It turned out, however, that the Irishman was deeply infected with a cutaneous eruption, which in some modern languages has been denominated "the itch." Osmer, resenting the exposure of himself and family to this vile disease, by the intrusion of this Hibernian, resolved on being revenged, and, at the same time, have something to relate which would secure him mirth at another time. Osmer, accordingly, restrained all appearance of resentment, and gravely told the fellow that he knew a sure remedy for his loathsome disease; but it was a secret, and he did not wish to divulge it. The poor fellow became very importunate for Osmer to prescribe for him, promising to follow the prescription to the letter, and swearing by the blessed Virgin that he would never reveal the secret. Osmer at length took the man out on to the meadow, where grew a forest of nettles, and told him if he would strip himself, and run through those weeds, it would insure him healing. No sooner said than done. Paddy went through them with a lion's heart; but his misery for a time was excruciating. This, together with the mortification of seeing how well Osmer enjoyed his suffering, opened his eyes to the fact that he had been imposed upon, and he immediately took up his line of march, calling on the Virgin to redress his wrongs. But this was not the last of it with Osmer. As soon as Osmer's neighbors were made acquainted with the fact, they dubbed *Doctor*, and he bore this adjunct title with him to the grave.

The next year, viz., in 1766, Samuel Sleeper and Benoni Wright came into Bradford, and pitched their tent a little north-east of Mr. Hunkins' dwelling, in the north part of Bradford, as I have already stated in my history of Newbury. In 1771, Andrew B. Peters, Esq., born in Hebron, Conn., January 29, 1764, came into this town. He came with his father to Thetford in 1766; in 1769, he moved into Piermont; and in 1771, he came into Bradford, at which time there were but ten families in the town.

Esquire Peters relates that the first grist-mill in the town was built by John Peters, in 1772, and that it stood on the south side of Wait's River, just above the bridge on the great river road. The first sawmill was built by Benjamin Baldwin, Esq., in 1774, and stood on Wait's River, where Baldwin's mills now stand, or did stand, a few years since. Esquire Peters relates a long-standing tradition, which went to account for the name *Wait* being given to the principal river of Bradford. It states that a man by the name of Wait belonged to Col. Rogers' party, which marched to the St. Francois in 1759; that this man and some others, in their hasty retreat, came upon the northern branch of Wait's River, and in a famishing state, they followed down this river in quest of game. Just as they entered what is now Bradford, Wait and one or two others proposed to go in advance of the rest, and see if they could not find something to satisfy their hunger. They had not gone but two or three miles before they shot a deer, and when they had satisfied their appetites, they hung up the rest of the savory meat upon a tree for the relief of their suffering companions in the rear; and that they might know who killed the deer, and for what purpose the meat was there suspended, Wait cut his name in the bark of the tree on which the meat hung. When the rear came up, and found the rich supply of food in readiness for them, they expressed their gratitude to Wait by giving his name to the stream they were then upon, and designed it as a remembrancer in all after-time, of the deliverance which was there wrought for them. There is nothing extravagant or unnatural in this narration ; and if the town cannot give a more satisfactory account of the origin of this name to their river, it may stand for the true one.

About sixty years ago, a little son of Absalom Fifield, who lived in the easterly part of Corinth, strayed from home, and was lost. As is usual in such cases, there was a very great excitement in the public mind, as well as in the minds of the parents, and multitudes went in search of the child. They sought for him unremittingly three days, and began to despair of the child, for they thought he must perish with hunger, if he was not already drowned, or devoured by wild beasts. But just at the close of the third day, he was discovered on an island in Wait's River, about five miles from the Connecticut, and three miles from his father's. When he was discovered, he was in company with a little lamb, and was picking tall blackberries, without any apparent anxiety. The boy was four or five years of age. He and the lamb were the only tenants of the island. They had contracted a friendship for each other, and the lamb followed in the footsteps of the boy wherever he went. But how either of them ever got on to the island remains a mystery.

The Rev. Gardner Kellogg was the first settled minister in the town—ordained, 1795; dismissed, 1809. The Rev. Silas McKeen was his successor; but I have not the date of his settlement or dismission. I might here notice some of the errors of

Thompson's Gazetteer in respect to the first settlers; but it is useless. There is no end to them.

PLYMOUTH, N. H.

I shall now pass into New Hampshire again, and state a few particulars in regard to the settlement of Plymouth, seeing it was one of the first towns settled in the county of Grafton, after Haverhill. This was the first town settled between Haverhill and Salisbury Lower Village. I received the following particulars from Samuel Dearborn, one of the first settlers, and from the Rev. Drury Fairbanks, who consulted the proprietors' records, and the church records, for my assistance. Samuel Dearborn originated in Old Chester, April 15th, 1745, and came into Plymouth, September, 1764. The two first families which came into the place, were Capt. James Hobart and Lieut. Zachariah Parker. They came from Hollis, N. H., in June, 1764. Hobart married Hannah Cummings, of Hollis, sister of the Rev. Dr. Cummings, of Billerica, Mass. Parker married Betsey Brown, of Hollis, niece of Benjamin Farley, Esq., late of Hollis. Hobart settled on Col. Edmunds' place, and Parker settled where Capt. Moses George did live, and perhaps does at this time. In September of this same year (1764), came Capt.

Jotham Cummings, Col. David Webster, Lieut. Josiah Brown, Ephraim Weston, James Blodgett, Deacon Stephen Webster, and Samuel Dearborn, all from Hollis, with the exception of Weston and Dearborn. At this time there was no bridge across any stream between Plymouth and Salisbury Lower Village, and no road but spotted trees. The first settlers from Hollis passed over the Merrimack into the town of Litchfield, and kept on the north side of the Merrimack until they came into the town of Holderness, and then crossed the Pemigewasset into Plymouth, a little south of Baker's River. Some of the early settlers of Haverhill and Newbury took the same route from Pembroke, kept on the north side of Baker's River, into Coventry, and then down the Oliverian.

The proprietors of the town of Plymouth voted at Hollis, April 16, 1764, "to hire Mr. Nathan Ward, of Newtown, Mass., to preach to the settlers at Plymouth, four days this spring;" this meant four Sabbaths. It appears that the proprietors expected that the settlement would be made sooner than it was; but Mr. Ward went on with the settlers, and preached the time specified, and dwelt with them in their tents. Mr. Ward received a call from them, which he accepted, and was ordained at Newburyport, in the meeting-house of the Rev. Jonathan Pearsons, July 10, 1765. At this time there were but eight families in the town of Plymouth. The proprietors voted to give the Rev. Mr. Ward *one hundred and fifty ounces of silver* for his salary, until there were one hundred families in the town, and then his salary was to be increased five ounces annually, until it amounted to *two hundred ounces*, and at that it was to remain as his permanent salary, with thirty cords of wood. He drew, also, one right of land, as the first settled• minister, and they voted him one hundred and twenty dollars, as an additional settlement. But what was the amount of Mr. Ward's salary? I find in Belknap's History of New Hampshire, vol. i. p. 151, in note, that an ounce of silver was estimated at six shillings and eight pence, lawful money; and accordingly, Mr. Ward's salary at the first was equal to one hundred and sixty-six dollars and fifty cents; and that at the last it amounted to two hundred and twenty-two dollars, exclusive of the wood. This, at first thought, was a limited salary for a minister. But upon a more thorough inspection of the matter, I think, we shall find it was better than most ministers receive at the present day. That money would purchase more bread-stuffs, taking one year with another, at that day, than twice, and perhaps thrice that amount, would purchase at this day. They had little, and next to *no* company. Their style of living was all different, and less expensive. Then he had a settlement, and a full right of land, which was enough to make two good farms. And I think we shall all agree that there is not a minister in the whole county of Grafton at this day, whose means of living from the people are as ample as were Mr. Ward's on the day of his settlement.

Mr. Ward labored in the ministry in Plymouth twenty-nine years; was dismissed April 22d, 1794; died in June, 1804, aged eighty-three. A man of God, and a great blessing to the town. Their first meeting-house was built of logs, and stood a little west of the Rev. Jonathan Ward's late dwelling-house, at the foot of the hill, east of the old meeting-house.

In April, 1765, Lydia Webster was born, daughter of Stephen and Lydia Webster. She was the first English child born in the town. At this birth, every woman was present in the town, and every husband attended his wife as far as the premises, and there remained until the vote was declared! This was a great day in Plymouth. That child is dead; but the mother was living with her third husband in Rumney, the last I heard from her. She was the wife of

Joseph Dearborn. Josiah Hobart was the first male child born in the town; but he is dead, also. These first settlers went to Concord, N. H., for their meal, for one or two years after they commenced their settlement, and drew it up on a hand-sled; but they soon raised an abundance, for their meadows were very fertile.

Ephraim Lund built the first saw and grist-mill near where Cochran's mills now are. Mr. Dearborn says that in 1765, James Heath, from Canterbury, Daniel Brainard, Esq., and Alexander Craig, made settlements in Rumney. Soon after, a Mr. Davis moved into Wentworth, and Joseph Patch into Warren. Mr. Dearborn says he knows that these were the first settlers in these towns, but will not be positive as to the year they made their entrance. Joseph Hobart was the first who settled in Hebron, and a Mr. Bennet first settled in Groton. Both of these towns were settled by people from Hollis. About the same time William Piper came into Holderness. It was certainly as late as 1765. The same year, Isaac Fox and a Mr. Taylor settled in Campton; and Benjamin Hoit from Old Chester settled Thornton in 1770.

Mr. Dearborn says that when Plymouth was first settled, and for some years, moose, bears, deer, and wolves were numerous. We may recollect that here Capt. Powers and his company "shot a moose," in 1754. Mr. Dearborn relates one anecdote of one Josiah Brown, who was famous for hunting at that early period of the settlement. He was well acquainted with Brown. He went out with snow-shoes. Hunter started some deer, and in the progress of the chase the deer crossed the river into New Hampton, and Brown attempted to follow; but in doing so where there was swift water, he broke through, and fell in up to his arms. He labored to throw himself on the ice; but the water had so much power upon his snow-shoes that his feet were carried down stream in an instant, and he would have to catch hold of the edge of the ice to keep himself from being drawn immediately under. Finding all his efforts ineffectual, and feeling himself nearly exhausted, he began to despair of life for more than a few minutes longer; but at this critical moment, who should appear but his true and faithful Hunter, who came directly up to him! Brown with one hand seized Hunter by the tail, and with the other he helped himself. Hunter drew for his life, and as the ice was rough, so that he had good foot-hold, he drew powerfully, and they both were enabled to overcome the force of the water, and Brown regained his standing upon the ice, happy in the reflection that both he and his anticipated game were still at liberty to make the best use of their feet.

Mr. Dearborn tells us an affecting story of a lost child in this town, in the time of the revolutionary war. A Mr. James Barnes sent his little son of seven or eight years of age, on an errand to a neighbor's; but he lost his way, and did not return at the time he was expected. The father went in pursuit of him, but not finding him, the neighbors were called on to go in search of him; and as the news spread that a child was lost, the whole town came together, and very many from other towns in the vicinity, and although the search was continued eight days, no trace of the child was ever discovered. It is very extraordinary, that if this child perished by hunger, his remains were never discovered; and if he was drowned, it seems that his body would have been ultimately found afloat. But the great day will disclose the facts in the case.

Much has been said in Plymouth and vicinity in respect to the naming of Baker's River. It was called Baker's River when the first settlers came on, and it was called so in the journal of Capt. Powers, in 1754. They have a tradition in the town, and they have always had from its first settlement, which explains the *how* and the *wherefore,* in this case. It is said that while Massachusetts was claiming the province of New Hampshire, prior to the old French war, Massachusetts sent a Capt. Baker, from Old Newbury, at the head of a company to ferret out the Indians, who had their encampment somewhere upon the waters of the Pemigewasset. Baker procured a friendly Indian who led them on to Plymouth. When Baker and his party had arrived on these meadows, the friendly Indian signified it was now time for every man to gird up his loins, and they did so, moving forward with all possible circumspection. When they had reached the south bank of Baker's River, near its junction with the Pemigewasset, they discovered the Indians on the north bank of Baker's River, sporting in great numbers, secure, as they supposed, from the muskets of all "pale faces." Baker and his men chose their position, and opened a tremendous fire upon the Indians, which was as sudden to them as a clap of thunder. Many of the sons of the forest fell in death in the midst of their sports. But the living disappeared in an instant, and ran to call in their hunters. Baker and his men lost no time in crossing the river in search of booty. They found a rich store of furs deposited in holes, dug into the bank of the river horizontally, in the manner bank-swallows make their holes. Having destroyed their wigwams, and captured their furs, Baker ordered a retreat, fearing that they would soon return in too great force to be resisted by his single company; and the Indians were fully up to his apprehensions—for notwithstanding Baker retreated with all expedition, the Indians collected, and were up with them, when they had reached a poplar plain in Bridgewater, a little south of Walter Webster's tavern. A smart skirmish ensued; but the Indians were repulsed with loss. Mr. Dearbon has visited that plain, and seen and examined a number of skulls, which he supposed fell in that engagement. One or two of them were perforated by a bullet. But notwithstanding the Indians were repulsed, the friendly Indian advised Baker and his men to use all diligence in their retreat, for he said their number would increase every hour, and that they would return to the attack. Accordingly, Baker pressed on the retreat, with all possible despatch, and did not allow his men to take refreshment after the battle. But when they came into New Chester, having crossed a stream, his men were exhausted through abstinence, forced marches, and hard fighting, and they resolved they would go no further without food, saying to their commander, "They might as well fall by the tomahawk as by famine." The captain acquiesced, and they prepared to refresh themselves; but here was a call for Indian stratagem. The friendly Indian told every man to build as many fires as he could in a given time; for the Indians, if they pursued them, would judge of their number by the number of their fires. He told them, also, that each man should make him four or five forks of crotched sticks, and use them all in roasting a single piece of pork; then leave an equal number of forks around each fire, and the Indians would infer, if they came up, that there were as many of the English as there were forks, and this might turn them back. The Indian's counsel was followed to the letter, and the company moved on with fresh speed. The Indians, however, came up while their fires were yet burning, and counting the fires and forks, the warriors whooped a retreat, for they were alarmed at the number of the English. Baker and his men were no longer annoyed by those troublesome attendants, and he attributed their preservation to the counsel of the friendly Indian. Now, it is said that Baker's River was so called, to perpetuate the brilliant affair, by Baker, at its mouth.

There was formerly another token of the presence or influence of a Mr. Baker, not very remotely connected with Baker's River. Salisbury was originally chartered by Massachusetts, prior to the old French war, and it was called *Bakerstown*. As this was the last chartered town in the direction from Massachusetts towards Plymouth, where Baker is said to have had his adventure, it would not be very unnatural for Massachusetts to honor his memory by calling this township after him.

The Rev. Drury Fairbanks was settled in Plymouth January 8, 1800, and was dismissed, March 18, 1818. Rev. Jonathan Ward was installed, August, 1818, and was dismissed about the year 1829.

I am now prepared to return to Haverhill and Newbury, and to relate some events which occurred there at a later period of their history. And as I have a sad tale to relate of the Indians, who lived at Coos for many years after the settlement by the English, I will here commence it.

I have already stated the evidence we have, that Newbury was an old Indian encampment, and that it was with great reluctance the Indians yielded up their interest in the Coos. That was a fatal step with the Indians, when they connected their destiny with that of the French; for they became identified with the enemy. They were greatly reduced in number, and when the French were subdued, the Indians fell with them, and they lost their remaining possessions, principally in New England. But after the old French war, there were some of the St. Francois tribe returned to the Coos, and lived until a more recent date, when they became entirely extinct.

Among those who returned, there were two families of special distinction—*John* and *Joe,* or *Captain* John, and *Captain* Joe, as they preferred to be called. John belonged to the St. Francois tribe, and had been a chief of some note with them. He was at the battle of Braddock's defeat, and used to relate how he shot a British officer, after he had been knocked down by the officer; and how he tried to shoot young Washington, but could not. He had repeatedly used the tomahawk and scalping knife upon the defenceless inhabitants of Massachusetts and New Hampshire; and when he was excited by spirit, he would relate his deeds of barbarity with fiendish satisfaction. He related how he mutilated a woman by cutting off her breasts, at the time of an assault upon the inhabitants near Fort Dummer, and he would imitate her shrieks and cries of distress. He was present at Boscawen, N. H., at the time the Indians surprised the inhabitants of that place. It must have been in 1746, or 1754. He related how they took an old woman, and as they found she could not travel as fast as they wished to retreat, he struck her on the head with a tomahawk, and he said she made a noise like a calf that is wounded on the head. He was a fierce and cruel Indian, and was the terror of the boys at Coos as long as he lived. He was, however, a staunch friend to the Colonies during the war of the revolution. He received a captain's commission, raised a part of a company of Indians, and marched with the Yankees against Burgoyne.

John had two sons—Pi-al, and Pi-al-Soosup,* both very different from their father in their disposition, being mild and inoffensive in their deportment. Pi-al-Soosup was in the company commanded by Capt. Thomas Johnson, near Fort Independence, in 1777, and as it was his first essay in arms, he was a good deal terrified when the battle commenced, on account of the tremendous roar of cannon from the fort and a British ship in the lake ; but as the firing from the ship and fort went over them, and did not much execution, except among the tops of the trees, Pi-al became reassured, and turning to Capt. Johnson, said, " Is this the way to fight ? " " Yes," said Johnson ; " fire ! fire !" " I say," said he, " this is good fun ; and, raising his gun, fired.

Captain Joe was a young man when he came to

---

* French sound of *i*, like *e*.

Coos. He belonged to a tribe in Nova Scotia; but when Louisburg was taken, his tribe was scattered when he was very young, and a remnant, he among the rest, made their way to the St. Francois tribe, and he grew up with them. This will show that there was some connection between the eastern Indians and those of the north; and it confirms the tradition with the Indians at Coos, that when their fathers heard of Lovewell's fight, they said, "They must soon leave Coössuck." Undoubtedly, Coossuck was the connecting link between Canada and all south and east in New England.

Joe was a very different character from John. He was aimiable, and never sought a quarrel. It used to be his boast, that he never "pointed the gun;" meaning, at his fellow man. Joe's wife went by the name of *Molly*, and she had two sons by a former husband when they came to Coos. The history of this affair is, that Joe was a great favorite among the fair daughters of St. Francois, and that Molly proved unfaithful to her first husband, and eloped with her two children, in order to enjoy the society of Joe in the States. Her sons' names were Toomalek and Muxa-Wuxal. Muxa-Wuxal died without causing Joe and Molly any more grief than they experienced in his loss; but it was far different with Toomalek.

He was literally a child for the fire. He was low in stature, wanting two inches of five feet, but had broad shoulders and haunches, and possessed extraordinary muscular powers. His thick, stiff hair grew down upon his forehead within one inch of his eyes, and his countenance was truly fiendlike. He had a murderous disposition, as the sequel will show. As he grew up, he became enamored of a young squaw, named Lewâ; but another Indian, named Mitchel, was his successful rival, and married Lewâ. But Toomalek determined on murdering Mitchel, and taking his wife. He accordingly prepared his gun, and watched for an opportunity to execute the horrid deed. It was not long before Toomalek discoverd Mitchel and his wife seated by a fire in the evening, at the upper end of the Ox Bow in Newbury, at the foot of the hill, just where the river turns north. They were seated side by side, happy for the present, and happy in anticipations, to all human view. Toomalek took aim, and discharged his gun at Mitchel; but Lewâ received the ball in her breast, and expired that evening. Mitchel was wounded, also, by the same ball which killed Lewâ, or there were two balls discharged; but he soon recovered from his wound. Toomalek was tried for his crime by his Indian peers, Old John presiding, and he was acquitted upon the ground that he did not mean to kill Lewâ, but *Mitchel*; and as he did not kill Mitchel, he was no murderer! This was making nice distinctions, and it shows that these untutored beings were adepts in the science of casuistry. But Old John was the sole means of his acquittal.

But Toomalek still cherished a rancorous enmity towards Mitchel, and his escape from justice, in the first instance, encouraged him to make a second attempt upon the life of Mitchel, who had taken another wife as attractive as Lewâ. Toomalek took a bottle of rum and a white man, Ebenezer Olmsted by name, and went to the wigwam of Mitchel, and commenced treating the compamy. Olmsted observed that Toomalek drank but little, whilst Mitchel indulged freely in his potations. When Mitchel began to be excited by the spirit he drank, he commenced upbraiding Toomalek for the murder of his wife, and for the wound inflicted on him. After much crimination and recrimination, promoted and aggravated by Toomalek for a specific purpose, Mitchel drew his knife upon his foe, and made a feeble pass at him. Toomalek then drew his knife on Mitchel, and gave him his death-wound at once! For this offence, Toomalek had his trial, and was acquitted, because Mitchel made the first assault, and

Toomalek argued that he killed Mitchel in self-defence; yet all were satisfied that Toomalek was the sole means of promoting the quarrel, and that he did it that he might have an excuse for killing Mitchel.

But Old John, who delighted in blood, was still using his influence to preserve the life of Toomalek; and he did it, as Providence overruled it, to bring upon himself and family a terrible calamity—nothing less than the murder of his elder son, Pi-al; and he did it on this wise. Toomalek, Pi-al, and several others were over on Haverhill side, and called at Charles Wheeler's house, son of Glazier Wheeler, on the little Ox Bow, about eleven o'clock in the forenoon. They were disposed to be somewhat noisy and turbulent at that time, and manifested that they had been drinking spirit. They asked for some there, but obtained none. They left Wheeler's before noon, and proceeded eastward. Some time in the afternoon, they came along near where the old courthouse stood in the north parish in Haverhill, west of Major Merrill's house, now Mr. Hibbard's, where they met a young squaw from Newbury, who began to rally Pi-al on some past acts of gallantry. Pi-al returned upon her measure for measure, which the young lady took in dudgeon. She could give, but not receive a joke. Perhaps Pi-al jested too near the truth. She turned aside, and held a brief conversation with Toomalek, in a low voice, and then passed on. Toomalek then stepped back to his companions, and walked south by the side of Pi-al; and in a few moments he drew his long knife, and by a back-hand stroke, plunged it into Pi-al's throat. It entered at the top of the sternum, and descended to the lungs. Pi-al ran with the blood spouting from the wound a few rods, and fell lifeless upon the ground. It was supposed that in this instance Toomalek killed Pi-al in obedience to the expressed wish of the young squaw; but he never criminated her. His companions ran and carried the news of the murder to their English neighbors, and Toomalek was taken into custody, without resistance, or an attempt to escape, and was carried across the river into Newbury, for his trial the next day. When the news came to Old John that Toomalek had killed his son Pi-al, he was overwhelmed with it, and his conscience awoke to its duty. He was almost frantic through agony. He confessed his sin in sparing the life of a murderer in the two previous instances already stated. He said, God had brought this calamity upon him for his sin; and both he and his wife spent the whole night in loud lamentations and self-reproaches.

The next day, in the forenoon, a court was called

to try Toomalek, and after all the evidence was obtained, they unanimously gave verdict against him, and said he must be shot. They appointed, however, a deputation to wait on the Rev. Mr. Powers, to know whether that decision was agreeable to the word of God. After hearing the evidence, he told them he believed it was, and they immediately set about carrying it into effect. By Indian law, Old John must be the executioner, as he was the nearest by blood to the slain, and he must avenge the blood of his son. The ground floor of the old court-house, standing opposite the burying ground at the west, was the place designated for the execution. Toomalek came to the place himself, without guard or attendance, where John stood in readiness with his loaded musket. He seated himself upon the floor, said his Catholic prayers, covered his eyes, and said, "Mack hence;" that is, "Kill me quick!" John stepped forward, put the muzzle of the gun near his head, and he was dead in an instant! Joe and Molly were both present at the execution of her son; and as soon as it was over, Joe took one arm, and Molly the other, and they dragged the body from the house and buried it. Molly had mourned and wept bitterly for the death of Muxa-Wuxal, which happened the same season; but she never shed a tear over the grave of Tomalek, nor was she ever heard to speak his name afterward. Old John was afterward found dead by the side of a log, at the foot of the hill, near the present garden of William Johnson.

Old Joe was a staunch whig, although he had no predilection for war himself. The "red coats" had broken up and dispersed his tribe in Nova Scotia, and he never would forgive them. He rejoiced in every success of the Colonies. He and Molly paid a visit to General Washington, at his head-quarters on North River, and he was received with marked attention. It was his boast to the last, that he had shook hands with Gen. Washington, and he and Molly were invited to sit at the general's table, after he and the other officers had eaten. And so great was his antipathy to the king of England, that he never would enter his dominions after the war. Some of his friends of the St. Francois tribe came down to Newbury on purpose to persuade him and Molly to return; but Captain Joe would hear nothing to it. He would take his hunting excursions at the extreme north of Vermont, but not pass into Canada. He and Molly went to Derby one season for a hunt, and built them a wigwam. The Indians of St. Francois heard of it, and came out and stole Molly when Joe was hunting, and carried her off to their quarters, in hopes that Joe would follow; but he would not. And having followed a moose two days in full expectation of taking him, when he came to find that the moose had crossed into Canada, he stopped short, and said—"Good bye, Mr. Moose!" turned upon his heel, and sought his repose in the states.

Joe and Molly have each a pond called after them in the town of Cabot. Joe's Pond empties itself into the Passumpsic by Joe's Brook. Molly's Pond discharges its waters into Lake Champlain by Onion River. Joe survived Molly many years. When he became old, and was unable to support himself, the legislature of Vermont voted him a pension of seventy dollars annually. He spent his last years with Mr. Frye Bailey, of Newbury. He departed this life, February 19, 1819, aged 79 years. Report made him much older than that; but it could not be true, if he was so young at the taking of Louisburg that he could not recollect the name of his tribe. At his funeral, the principal men of the town attended. He was buried in the south-eastern corner of the burying ground. His gun, which was found loaded after his death, was discharged over his grave. His snow-shoes are with Mr. Frye Bailey. With Capt. Joe fell the last of the Indians at Coössuck, that once fairy land of long-slumbering generations!

We have already spoken of the war of the revolution when upon individual character, fortified houses, and commanders of companies, &c. But these times require more distinct consideration in these annals, because they form an epoch in our history; and because they embrace many things which serve to develop causes which for a long period have lain concealed from general observation; which causes cannot fail to interest the descendants of those who bore the burden and heat of the day in which our independence was achieved. The first settlers at Coos sustained, in common with their brethren, all the hardships which were brought on the Colonies by the war of the revolution; and, owing to their peculiar circumstances, they were called to additional burdens, almost too grievous to be borne. They were yet struggling with the privations and inconveniences necessarily attendant upon new settlements, remote from old towns and a ready market. They were frontier settlements. They were contiguous to the strongholds of the enemy, and were continually exposed to their savage incursions. And what was worst of all, Vermont was not an acknowledged state, although she had often requested to be received into the Union. This was owing to conflicting claims to these Grants, set up by the states of New York, New Hampshire, and Massachusetts. No two of them could agree who should have them, yet all could agree to oppose in Congress the admission of Vermont into the Union as an independent state ; and so influential were those three states at that time, that Congress did not dare to decide contrary to their wishes, although they might see manifest injustice in their opposition. The British were fully aware of the excited state of feeling in Vermont in regard to this subject, and as Vermont was rejected by her sister Colonies, they entertained strong hopes that they should detach her from the common interest of the Colonies, and bring her to espouse the cause of the mother country. To this end the British made every possible effort by promises and threats. Their scouts traversed the whole territory, promising the most liberal rewards to all who would befriend them, and threatening vengeance upon the lives and property of those who should adhere to the interest of the Colonies.

Vermont had a difficult part to sustain in the grand drama then being acted. She stood between two or more fires, and it required all her physical powers, and all her finesse, not to founder in Scylla or Charybdis. The alluring promises of the British had actually brought many to feel favorably inclined to their cause, and it is thought that there were some of this description in high places. Others would listen to these proposals of the British for self-preservation; for now these Grants were left to repel all invasions single handed. It was also true that tories from other states sought a retreat in the Grants, where they were less liable to arrest, and where they could with greater facility maintain correspondence with the British. And so it was, that the British came in possession of all the movements of the Americans, as soon as any plan was matured against the enemy. But we ought here to state that there were many true-hearted Americans in the Grants; men who were ready to sacrifice their property and to lay down their lives in defense of their country; and those who took the field did nobly, and by their heroic deeds, they gained the distinctive appellation, *the Green Mountain Boys*, a title which their descendants are proud to bear to this day.

The policy which the leading men of that day adopted was, not to declare, either that they would or would not be independent of the mother country; intending thereby to save themselves from an invasion by the British, and, at the same time, to present motives to Congress for receiving them into the Union. This was a difficult part to perform, owing to the ardor with which the British pressed the subject for an immediate decision ; but it was maintained, and Vermont finally secured her utmost wishes.

But while these things were transacting, there were men, in almost every town, who had rendered themselves very obnoxious to the displeasure of the British and tories, and they were unwearied in their endeavors to get them into their hands. The tories were relied upon by the British for those captures, and they were by far the most dangerous foe that our men had to contend with. They would intrude themselves into the families of the whigs under the mask of friendship, draw forth the secrets of their breasts, convey them to the British, and then lead on a scouting party to the threshold of their neighbor, or, in his absence, kill his cattle or set fire to his dwelling in the dead hour of night. We can hardly conceive how distressing such a state of suspense and watchful anxiety must have been during the long period of eight years. But Newbury was annoyed by these means far more than Haverhill, for those scouts of the enemy had not the temerity to cross the river, well knowing that a retreat would be next to impossible.

There were several men in Newbury who had, by their devotion to their country, excited the enmity of the British and tories to a high degree, and they were resolved on taking them. One was the Rev. Peter Powers, who had preached and done everything in his power to sustain the cause of the Colonies, and he had already buried his oldest son, Peter, in the army. But, as I have previously stated, Mr. Powers moved on to Haverhill side for his security. Gen. Jacob Bailey was another of these men. He was a very prominent man at that day. He possessed great influence with his countrymen, and the Indians looked up to him as a father. He acted as quartermaster-general to the troops stationed at Newbury and in the vicinity, and the Indians were not overlooked in the distribution of the daily rations. He retained their friendship during the war. The British felt it so important to secure Gen. Bailey, that they offered a heavy reward for his person, and many plans were concerted for his capture; but they never succeeded. Col. Thomas Johnson was another man whom they considered as a notorious rebel, as he had distinguished himself at the taking of Ticonderoga and the seige of Mount Independence, in the autumn of 1777. At that time, Johnson went out as captain of a volunteer company from Newbury; but he acted, a part of the time, as aid to Gen. Lincoln. When the British surrendered at Ticonderoga, one hundred of the prisoners were given in charge to Col. Johnson, and he marched them back into the country, where they would not be exposed to a recapture, and where they would not diminish the rations of our men at the fort. The British, of course, were desirous of taking Col. Johnson; but he eluded all their vigilance until the spring of 1781, when they succeeded in capturing him. It was on this wise. Col. Johnson had contracted to build a grist-mill in Peacham, and when he went up with the mill-stones in March, he put up at the house of Deacon Jonathan Elkins, in Peacham, which house was surrounded in the night by some British and tories, was broken open, and Johnson, Jacob Page, Jonathan and Moses Elkins, sons of Deacon Elkins, were taken prisoners. But as I have Col. Johnson's journal of this date, it may be more interesting to give the journal itself.

"*March* 5, 1781. This morning early, went over to Haverhill with my teams for my mill-stones. Returned before dinner, shod my oxen, took dinner, and set out for Peacham at 2 P. M. This night put up at Orr's, in Ryegate.

Tuesday, 6th. This day, being thawy and bad going, I was obliged to leave one of my mill-stones within one mile of the place where we lodged. This night arrived at Peacham with the other mill-stone. Lodged at Mr. Elkins'.

"*Wednesday*, 7th. This morning, finding my oxen lame, I sent Mr. Josiah Page, with the oxen, home. Hired Jonathan Elkins, with his oxen, and went back and took the other mill-stone, and returned to Peacham. Should have returned home myself this evening, but was a little unwell.

"*Thursday*, 8th. This morning, about twelve or one o'clock, I awaked out of my sleep, and found the house beset with enemies. Thought I would slip on my stockings, jump out of the window, and run. But before that, came in two men with their guns pointed at me, and challenged me for their prisoner, but did not find myself the least terrified. Soon found two of the men old acquaintances of mine. I saw some motions for tying me, but I told them that I submitted myself a prisoner, and would offer no abuse. Soon packed up, and marched, but never saw people so surprised as the family was. When we came to Mr. Davis', I found the party to consist of eleven men, Capt. Prichard commanding. Then marched seven or eight miles, when daylight began to appear. I found Moses Elkins looked very pale. I told the captain he had better let him go back, for he was drowned when he was small, and that he would not live through the woods. He said he would try him further; but on my pleading the pity it would be to lose such a youngster, he sent him back. We soon halted for refreshment. To my great surprise, I found John Gibson and Barlow of the party. Then marched about four miles, and obtained leave to write a letter and leave on a tree, then marched. I was most terribly tired and faint. Camped down on the River Lamoille this night.

"*Friday*, 9th. This day marched down the River Lamoille, about twelve miles below the forks. One of the finest countries of land that ever I saw. Camped about eleven o'clock at night.

"*Saturday*, 10th. This day marched to the lake. Underwent a great deal by being faint and tired. The captain and men were very kind to us. A stormy and uncomfortable night.

"*Sunday*, 11th. This morning went on to the lake ten miles, north of the mouth of the River Lamoille; marched fifteen miles on the lake, then crossed the Grand Isle; marched ten miles to Point Au Fer. Dinner being on the table, I dined with the commandant of that fort, and supped with him. Was well treated.

"*Monday*, 12th. This day marched to the Isle Au Noix, went into the fort, into a barrack, got a cooking; but the commandant ordered the prisoners out of the fort to a block-house; but soon had sent me a good dinner and a bottle of wine. Then Capt. Sherwood called on me to examine me. In the evening, Capt. Sherwood and Capt. Prichard waited on me to Mr. Jones, where we drinked a bottle of wine. Capt. Prichard and I slept there.

"*Tuesday*, 13th. This day marched to St. John's. Col. St. Leger took me to his house, and gave me a shirt, gave me some refreshment, which I much needed. Told me I was to dine with him. Major Rogers and Esq. Marsh and others dined there. Then gave me my parole, which I am told is the first instance of a prisoner having his parole in this fort without some confinement. Lodged with Esq. Marsh.

"*Wednesday*, 14th. This morning, Esquire Marsh and I were invited to Capt. Sherwood's to breakfast. Then Capt. Sherwood took charge of me, and I lived with him. To my great satisfaction, this evening came Mr. Spardain to see me, who was a prisoner to me at *Ti.* He said, on hearing that I was a prisoner, he went to the commandant to inform him of the good treatment he and others had from me while they were prisoners to me. The commandant sent him to my quarters to inform me that my good treatment of them was much to my advantage."

In this same journal, under date of June 14th, we

have the colonel's impressions from witnessing a Roman Catholic procession, and his views of the Canadians. He was at this time at Three Rivers.

"*June* 14th. This day there was a Roman Catholic procession. Their walks, their shows, very extraordinary. Their carrying God Almighty about the streets is something new to me. I think it is a curse to the land, and a curse to their king, to have such a miserable set of inhabitants as these Canadians. They are the most ignorant, superstitious, idle, and careless set of people that can be thought of, spending half of their time in holidays and going to mass. The women wear riding-hoods the hottest weather."

This journal of Col. Johnson will show clearly the policy of the British towards different individuals of the Grants, treating those of some distinction with great urbanity and kindness, in hopes of winning them over to their cause, and treating others with needless severity. Col. Johnson was treated with marked attention during his whole stay in Canada; but it fared differently with Page and Elkins. Johnson was for some time kept at St. John's, and was allowed his parole—not a parole to go where he pleased, but a parole known in the military profession, which distinguishes between friends and enemies in camp; and it is a privilege granted to certain individuals every day, and proclamation of it is made every day by a certain officer.

Page was sent directly down to Montreal, and we never hear of him afterwards. Jonathan Elkins was carried directly down to Quebec, and was there imprisoned, and suffered immensely from want until late in the fall of 1781, when he and one hundred and fifty others were put on board a ship and sent to England, where they were confined in Mill Prison from February 9, 1782, till the 24th of June following. They had but two-thirds the allowance of a common soldier, and they were miserably clad, most of them. Dr. Franklin, who was then our minister at France, hearing of their poor condition, sent each prisoner one shilling sterling per week, in addition to their allowance from the British government, and this was a great relief to them. Col. Elkins says to me under his own hand—"There were among us forty captains of vessels, and many others who had some learning; and when we got our shilling a week from Dr. Franklin, it was proposed that we, who had no learning, should pay four coppers a week for schooling, and soon many schools were opened. Among the rest, I procured paper, pen and ink, and a slate, and paid my four coppers per week for tuition. By this means, many who could neither read nor write, got so much learning, that they were capable of transacting business for themselves, and a number of us learned the mariner's art, so as to be capable of navigating a ship. On the 24th of June, 1782, there were one thousand seven hundred and thirty-three prisoners put on board a cartel, and sent to America in exchange for Lord Cornwallis' grenadiers and light infantry. And I returned with them to my native country.

"JONATHAN ELKINS.

"Peacham, Vt., Dec. 8, 1832."

We return again to see how it resulted with Johnson. Notwithstanding Johnson was treated with so much apparent respect, he could not but observe that he had his quarters often shifted from St. John's to Montreal, then to Chambly, then to Three Rivers, and at each place he would be interrogated by different officers relative to the views and feelings of the inhabitants of the Grants, and what he thought of the prospects of the Colonies. To all these and similar inquiries he replied with as much apparent indifference to the cause of America as he could show, never relating to them an untruth, and still reserving to himself whatever he thought might be advantageous to them, and detrimental to America. And he had cause to congratulate himself for having adhered to this uniform course; for he found out, after a while, that all his conversation with these different officers, at different places, was penned down and sent to the supreme commandant, to be inspected by him, to see if his statements agreed. He caught the reading of a note, also, which was sent from one in high command to the young officer who had the charge of him. The purport of it was this—"I take you to be a person of too much sense and intelligence to be imposed upon by the prisoner." The young man's sense and intelligence were not enough to restrain him from occasional hard drinking, and at one of those seasons, he left this note exposed to Johnson's inspection. These things taught Johnson that after all their show of confidence in him, they were still suspicious of him; and he thought, if they were disposed to play Yankee with him, he would take a game with them at that. He accordingly affected more and more indifference to the cause of the Colonies; until they began to feel that if he was in other circumstances, he would render them essential service. Accordingly, after retaining him between seven and eight months, they told Johnson if he would give them information of the movements of the Americans, supply their scouts with provision if called upon, and return to them when they demanded, he might return home upon his parole. Johnson assented to these stipulations, and signed the following instrument : —

"I, Lieut. Col. Johnson, now at . John's, do hereby pledge my faith and word of honor to his excellency, Gen. Holdimand, whose permission I have obtained to go home, that I shall not do or say any thing contrary to his majesty's interest or government; and that whenever required so to do, I shall repair to whatever place his excellency or any other his majesty's commander-in-chief in America shall judge expedient to order me, until I shall be legally exchanged, and such other person as shall be agreed upon, sent in my place.

"Given under my hand at St. John's, this fifth day of October, one thousand seven hundred and eighty-one.

"Col. THOMAS JOHNSON."

Upon Col. Johnson's signing this instrument, he returned home to his family at Newbury, and neither received any intelligence from the British, nor gave any, until January following, as we learn from a communication of Col. Johnson to Gen. Washington, bearing date, May 30, 1782. In January, Col. Johnson received a letter from Capt. Prichard, by the hand of Levi Sylvester, of Newbury, and one from George Smith, in Canada. In February, 1782, Col. Johnson wrote a letter to Gen. Holdimand and one to Prichard, and sent them by Sylvester. He sent, also, two newspapers containing the account of the surrender of Lord Cornwallis. A copy of those letters was sent to Gen. Washington the May following, and a copy of Smith's letter to Johnson was also enclosed. Sylvester informed Col. Johnson that Major Rogers had come into the Grants at the head of a strong scout, and was then at Mooretown, now Bradford, and wished to see him that night; but Johnson was detained, and did not go until some days after, and then he did not find Rogers, and did not see him at all.

At this time Col. Johnson feeling oppressed with his peculiar situation, being liable, on the one hand, to be viewed and treated as a traitor by the British, and on the other, to be numbered with the enemies of his country, determined to communicate to Gen. Washington all he had learned in his captivity, all he had done to obtain his liberty, and all he had done from the time of his leaving Canada, and his *motives* for doing so, and solicit the general's advice in respect to the course he had better pursue. He accordingly wrote a detailed account, covering about nine pages of common-sized paper, too long to be inserted in these sketches, agreeing, to wonderful exactness, with the statement the colonel made to me, near the close of life, although he did not know at that time that a single line of it was in existence, and expressed the deepest regret that he had not kept copies of his letters to Washington, and of Washington's letter to him. They have, however, since come to light, having been found among Washington's private papers, and are now in the possession of the Rev. Jared Sparks, of Cambridge, Mass., and have been by him transcribed and certified, at the request of Mr. David Johnson, of Newbury. This first paper to which I allude is an interesting document, and, would my limits permit, I should be pleased to give it entire to my readers; but the letter accompanying, and those which followed this communication, will explain this whole affair, and revive many interesting facts which have lain dormant, perhaps, in the minds of the aged for many years. The letter accompanying the document bears the same date of the document itself, and is as follows:

9*

"THOS. JOHNSON TO GEN. WASHINGTON.

"Newbury, 30 May, 1782.

"May it please your excellency to indulge me while I say, that in the month of March, 1781, I was taken a prisoner, as set forth in my narrative, continued in Canada until September, when I obtained liberty to return home on parole, which I could effect only by engaging to carry on a correspondence with them. This was my view, to get what intelligence I was able respecting their plans and movements, and in hopes to be exchanged, that I might be able, in a regular way, to have given some important intelligence. I have taken such measures as appeared most likely to effect the same; but as these have hitherto failed, I find the season so far advanced as not to admit of further delay without acquainting your excellency.

"The proposed plans of the enemy for the last campaign were frustrated for want of provisions; but they determined to pursue them this spring as early as possible. To this end, they have used their most unwearied endeavors with Vermont to prepare the way, which they have, in a great and incredible degree, brought to pass, and is daily increasing; and unless some speedy stop is put to it, I dread the consequences. I entreat your excellency, that if possible, by a regular exchange, I may be enabled to give all the intelligence in my power without hazarding my character, which, otherwise, I am determined to do, at the risk of my honor, my all—and, perhaps, to the great injury of hundreds of poor prisoners now in their hands. Having had experience, I am grieved to think of their situation. This infernal plan of treachery with Vermont (as I have often heard in Canada) was contrived before Ethan Allen left the British, and he was engaged on their side. It ran through the country like a torrent, from New York to Canada, and the present temper of Vermont is a piece of the same. Were the people in general upon the Grants, on this side the mountains, to declare for New Hampshire or New York, it would be contrary to the agreement of their leading men ; and, unless protected by your excellency, the innocent with the guilty would share a miserable fate. This part of the country being sold by a few designing men, of whom a large number are very jealous, a small number have by me their informer, or otherwise, got the certainty of it, and it puts them in a most disagreeable situation. They are desirous of declaring for New Hampshire ; but many of their leaders earnestly dissuading them from it, it keeps us in a tumult, and I fear the enemy will get so great an advantage as to raise their standard to the destruction of this part of the country. They keep their spies constantly in this quarter without molestation, and know every movement, and transmit the same directly to Canada ; and when matters take a turn contrary to their minds, we are miserably exposed to their severest resentment. I am entirely devoted to your excellency's pleasure. Should my past conduct meet your excellency's approbation, my highest ambition will be satisfied ; if not, deal with me as your wisdom shall dictate. I most earnestly entreat your excellency to meditate a moment on my critical and perplexing situation, as well as that of this part of the country, and that I may receive by Capt. Bailey, the bearer, who will be able to give you further information, your excellency's pleasure in this affair. I beg leave to subscribe myself your excellency's most sincere and most devoted servant.

"THOS. JOHNSON."

Col. Johnson stated in this letter what he verily believed to be true of the men in the Grants, who were carrying on a correspondence with the British. He viewed it just as it was viewed by the British, and he had no means of knowing any thing to the contrary ; but it ultimately appeared that some of these men, who were considered friends to the British, were playing a deep game, in which the British, the Continental Congress, and themselves, were distinct parties. These men were determined that Vermont should be a distinct and independent community, like the other states; but as Congress would not receive them, and had withdrawn their troops that had been sent for their defence, they managed as they could with the British to preserve the Grants from invasion. There is no doubt but the British were completely deceived by them, and Ethan Allen procured an engagement, on the part of the British, that no hostilities should be carried on against Vermont. The principal men in this understanding were Thomas Chittenden, Moses Robinson, Samuel Safford, Ethan Allen, Ira Allen, Timothy Brownson, John Fasset, and Joseph Fay. But at the same time, the British correspondence, with them was transmitted to Congress, by these men, to operate as an inducement for Congress to receive them into the Union, and Ethan Allen wrote to Congress in the following bold and impassioned language :—"I am resolutely determined to defend the independence of Vermont, as Congress are that of the United States, and rather than fail, will retire with the hardy Green Mountain Boys into the caverns of the mountains, and wage war with human nature at large." But surely there was enough seen and heard in Canada, at the time Col. Johnson was prisoner there, to make any friend of his country tremble for the consequences. But we have Gen. Washington's answer to Col. Johnson's letter of the 30th May, 1782.

" *To Capt. Thomas Johnson, Exeter, N. H.*

Head-Quarters, 14 June, 1782.

" Sir,

" I have received your favor per Capt. Bailey, and thank you for the information contained, and would beg you to continue your communication whenever you shall collect any intelligence you shall think of importance. It would give me real pleasure to have it in my power to effect your exchange ; but some unhappy circumstances have lately taken place, which, for the present, cut off all exchange. If you can fall upon any mode to accomplish your wishes, in which I can with propriety give you my assistance, I shall be very glad to afford it.

I am, sir, &c.

" G. WASHINGTON."

"THOS JOHSON TO GEN. WASHINGTON.

Exeter, July 20, 1782.

" I am obliged by your excellency's favor of the 14th June, to acknowledge your excellency's goodness in offering your assistance in my exchange. I think it proper to give a more particular account of my situation, and have enclosed a copy of my parole for your perusal. I think, agreeable to the parole, they cannot refuse a man in my room, although there is no exchange agreed upon. Your excellency will determine on my rank. I was held at Canada a lieutenant-colonel in the militia. I was a captain, and afterwards chosen a lieutenant-colonel in the militia, agreeable to the order of the Assembly of New York; but being at a great distance, before my commission could reach me, Vermont claimed jurisdiction, and I never had the commission, and I told them the same; but I was obliged to acknowledge myself as such in my parole, or I could not have accomplished my design. My situation grows more distressing. I have been exposed by the infirmity or imprudence of a gentleman, one that we could not have expected it from. I have received nothing of much importance since my last. I have since received a confirmation of their intentions to execute rigorous measures againt the opposers of Vermont. I have fears of an invasion on that part of New Hampshire by the imprudence above mentioned. I have fears of the correspondence being stopped; have wrote to Canada; since which, by agreement, Capt. Prichard was to meet on Onion River, the 10th of this instant. Private concerns brought me here at this time. If suspicion don't prevent, I expect something of importance waiting for me; should it prevent, shall stand in the greatest need of a man to send in exchange for me.

"I am, sir, your most humble servant,

"THOS. JOHNSON."

We have another letter from Col. Johnson to Gen. Washington, dated at Atkinson, N. H., September 20, 1782. This is a letter of four pages, and as it differs not materially from the two former, I omit it in these sketches.

I give place to a letter of Meshech Weare to Gen. Washington on the subject of Col. Johnson's peculiar circumstances. This Mr. Weare was governor of New Hampshire in 1784.

"MESHECH WEARE TO GEN. WASHINGTON.

"Hampton Falls, Nov. 25, 1782.

"Sir,

"The bearer, Col. Thomas Johnson, of whose conduct with respect to procuring intelligence from the enemy, your excellency has been informed, now waits on you to communicate some things which appear to be important. From every information I have been able to obtain, I have no reason to suspect his honesty or fidelity. His situation at this time is very difficult, as he will fully inform you, and requests your assistance in such way as you may think proper. I cannot help expressing my fears of what may be the consequence of the negotiations carrying on between Vermont and Canada, of which there seems now to be scarce a doubt.

"I have the honor to be, with the greatest respect, yours, &c.

"MESHECH WEARE."

We have one other interesting letter on this subject. It is from Nathaniel Peabody, of Atkinson, N. H. Mr. Peabody was a member of the council in New Hampshire, in 1785, and subsequently a member of Congress.

"NATH. PEABODY TO GEN. WASHINGTON.

"Atkinson, State of New Hampshire,
Nov. 27, 1782.

"Sir—I take the liberty to address your excellency respecting the unhappy situation of Lieut. Col. Johnson, of Newbury, Coos, who will take charge of this letter, and do himself the honor to wait on your excellency in person. Col. Johnson is desirous of giving to your excellency every information in his power, relative to the situation, strength, and designs of the enemy at the northward, the embarrassed state of affairs in the country where he lives, and more particularly the ineligible circumstances in which his own person, family, and domestic concerns are unhappily involved.

"I have no doubt he hath been ungenerously deceived, injured, and betrayed by some persons with whom he found it necessary to intrust certain secrets, to him of great importance, and from whom he had a claim to better treatment.

"The latter end of last month I received a letter from Col. Johnson, the contents of which he will make known to you ; and I should have then done myself the honor of transmitting the same, with some other information, to your excellency ; but on a conference I had with the president of this state, it was concluded that intrusting affairs of that nature by common post-riders would be unsafe for the public, and dangerous for Col. Johnson, and that it was expedient to despatch an express on purpose, as it was adjudged probable your excellency had such a variety of other channels for information, that there was little prospect of giving new and important intelligence. From the best information I have been able to obtain, my own observation, and the personal knowledge I have had for some years past, of Col. Johnson, I am led without hesitating to conclude that he is a faithful and sincere friend to the independence of these United States ; that he would contribute every thing in his power to promote the political salvation of this, his native country ; and that he is a gentleman on whose declaration your excellency may place full dependence.

"I have the honor to be yours, &c.

"NATH. PEABODY."

The above has been copied from the originals now in my possession.

JARED SPARKS.

Cambridge, Sept. 17, 1835.

There is nothing on paper to show the result of Col. Johnson's interview with Gen. Washington ; but it is well known with what feeling and interest the colonel related the particulars of that interview until the close of life. It is not probable that Gen. Washington was at that time in circumstances to effect an exchange of prisoners, so as to set Johnson at liberty, nor does this seem to be the main object of his visit ; but he obtained the full approbation of Washington, and enjoyed his sympathies, as he had previously expressed in his letter. But the treaty of peace, which was signed on the 20th of January, 1783, in less than two months after Col. Johnson's visit to Washington, set Johnson at liberty, dissipated all anxieties, and conveyed peace and independence to the states.

I have given place to the preceding documents for two reasons : one is, they give the present generation a more lively and distinct idea of the trials and dangers which the inhabitants of Coos sustained in the revolutionary struggle, than any general history of those times gives, or can give ; the other is, to do justice to the injured. All know what aspersions were heaped upon Col. Johnson for the part he was said to perform at that eventful period, and what pain it inflicted on him through life, although conscious of innocence in respect to those charges. He supposed time and Providence had forever deprived him of the means to demonstrate his innocence ; and under this apprehension, he resigned this life, January 4th, 1819, aged seventy-seven years. But it seems that Providence designed ultimately to refute all those charges ; and what God undertakes is thoroughly done. If ever mortal man was vindicated in any supposed case, and his character set above all suspicion, that man is Col. Thomas Johnson, touching his patriotism in the day that tried men's souls.

I have already stated how desirable an object it was

with the British to get in possession of Gen. Jacob Bailey. A bold and determined effort to effect this was made on the 17th of June, 1782, while Col. Johnson was at home on parole. Gen. Bailey lived at the Johnson village, in a house where now stands the brick house of Josiah Little. Capt. Prichard and his scout, to the number of eighteen men, lay upon the heights west of the Ox Bow, and they made a signal for Col. Johnson to visit them. Johnson went, as he was bound to do by the terms of his parole, and he learned that they had come to capture Gen. Bailey that evening. Johnson was now in a great strait. Bailey was his neighbor, and a host against the enemy, and Johnson could not have him go into captivity; and yet he must seem to conform to the wishes of Prichard, or he would be recalled to Canada himself, and in all probability have his buildings laid in ashes. Johnson returned to his house, and resolved to inform Bailey of his danger, at the hazard of every thing to himself. But how was this to be done? Bailey, with two of his sons, was ploughing on the Ox Bow. Prichard's elevated situation on the hill enabled him to look down upon the Ox Bow as upon a map. The secret was intrusted to Dudley Carleton, Esq., the brother of Col. Johnson's wife. Johnson wrote on a slip of paper this laconic sentence—"The Philistines be upon thee, Sampson!" He gave it to Carleton, and instructed him to go on to the meadow, pass directly by Bailey without stopping or speaking, but drop the paper in his view, and return home by a circuitous rout. Carleton performed the duty assigned him well. Gen. Bailey, when he came to the paper, carelessly took the paper and read it, and as soon as he could, without exciting suspicion in the minds of lookers on, proposed to turn out the team, and said to his sons, "Boys, take care of yourselves!" and went himself down to the bank of the river, and the sons went up to the house, to carry the tidings to the guard that was stationed there. The guard consisted of Capt. Frye Bailey, commandant, Ezra Gates, Jacob Bailey, Jun., Joshua Bailey, Sergeant Samuel Torrey, a hired man of Gen. Bailey, three boys—John Bailey, Isaac Bailey, and Thomas Metcalf—and a hired maid, Sarah Fowler.

Although the guard was apprised of the general's apprehensions, yet it would seem they thought his fears were groundless, for they were taken by surprise at early twilight, while they were taking their evening grog; or, we might more significantly say, perhaps, that they were taking in a freight of *prowess* to be tested at a late hour of the night. The enemy were not discovered until they were within a few rods of the front door. Sergeant Torrey met them at the door, and levelled his piece at them ; but Prichard knocked aside the gun, made Torrey his prisoner, and the enemy rushed in. The guard dispersed in all directions. Ezra Gates was wounded in the arm by a ball, as he ran from the south front door, and a gun was discharged at John Bailey, as he was jumping the fence to run for the Ox Bow, and two balls lodged in the fence close to him. Thomas Metcalf reached the meadow, where he tarried all night. Gates was brought in and laid on the bed, where he lay bleeding and groaning, whilst the enemy were searching the house for prisoners and papers.

But there was one belonging to the house, who displayed great presence of mind and intrepidity. It was woman ! woman, who in ten thousand instances, has risen superior to danger, and performed astonishing deeds of heroism, when man, her lord by constitution, has forfeited his claim to superiority by timidity and flight ! Sarah Fowler, the servant-maid spoken of, remained upon the ground with a babe of Mrs. Bailey in her arms, undismayed at the sight of loaded muskets and bristling bayonets, and repeatedly extinguished a candle, which had been lighted for the purpose of searching the house. Not succeeding with a candle, one of the party took a firebrand, and attempted to renew the search; this the dauntless maid struck from his hand, and strewed the coals around the room. This was too much for British blood; and one of the soldiers swore, by a tremendous oath, that if she annoyed them any more, he would blow out her brains, showing at the same time how he would do it. She then desisted, as she had good reason to believe he would execute his threat.

Mrs. Bailey had, at the moment of the onset, escaped through an eastern window, and lay concealed in currant bushes in the garden. The enemy, having destroyed one gun, and taken what papers they could find, commenced their retreat, greatly disappointed in respect to the main object of their pursuit, for the general was resting securely on Haverhill side. They took with them prisoners, Gates and Pike, the hired man of Gen. Bailey, and proceeded south. An alarm was given, but not in time to arrest the enemy. About a half a mile south, they met James Bailey, son of Gen. Bailey, whom they took prisoner, and kept until the close of the war. They took also Pelatiah Bliss, who lived near where Harry C. Bailey now lives. Bliss whined and cried, and made so much ado about his wife and babes, and exhibited so many symptoms of a weak mind, that, after consultation, they permitted him to escape. They called at one other house, Andrew Carter's, drank all the pans of milk the old lady had, and then prosecuted their march into Canada, to report the failure of their expedition. "But," says Col. Elkins, of Peacham, in his letter of December 7, 1832, "this failure of the British, in the main object of their expedition, brought fresh trouble upon Col. Thomas Johnson. The tories in the vicinity, who had laid the plan for taking Gen. Bailey, learning that he was not at home that night, and knowing that he was not in the habit of being absent from his family over night, unless on business out of town, said at once, Johnson was a traitor to their cause, for he must have given Bailey information of his danger. This rumor went with the party back to Canada, and produced strong sensations of jealousy and resentment there. Johnson was now the man to be obtained, and his buildings were to be destroyed by fire the next spring, if not before. But the disposition to peace in the mother country, and the actual treaty before the year came about, saved Johnson from the calamities threatened upon him.

From this time the people of Coos moved on in the even tenor of their way to ease and independence in their circumstances. But even at the late period of which we have been speaking, a one-horse pleasure carriage had never been seen at Coos. The first that was ever seen in Newbury, was brought into the place by a Rev. Mr. Goddard, who was preaching as a candidate to the people there, after the dismission of the Rev. Mr. Powers. He rode up to Gen. Bailey's, as he came into town, in a chaise or sulkey. There was living at the general's a young miss, who happened to be in at a neighboring house to visit an aunt, at the time Mr. Goddard passed. So strange a vehicle greatly excited her curiosity, and she called out to her aunt, "O, come here, aunt! come here, and see a man riding in a cart with two tongues!" On horseback in summer, and in sleighs in winter, were the only methods of riding at that day.

I have previously said that Haverhill and Newbury were never one ecclesiastical society after the dismission of the Rev. Mr. Powers. The Rev. Jacob Wood was the successor of Mr. Powers in Newbury. He was ordained on the second Wednesday in January, 1788; departed this life, February 10, 1790, aged 33. Rev. Nathaniel Lambert was ordained, November 17, 1790; dismissed April 4, 1809. Rev. Luther Jewett was ordained, February 28, 1821; ceased to officiate, February 3, 1825; dismissed, February 19, 1828.

Rev. Clark Perry was ordained, June 4, 1828; dismissed, June 15, 1835. Rev. George Campbell was installed, January 27, 1836, and remains their pastor. Let us hope for a long, successful, and happy union.

From the time Mr. Powers closed his labors at Haverhill, the people enjoyed but little preaching until the year 1790. There was no organized church in Haverhill, as they had belonged to Newbury church, and there were but two males, members of Newbury church, who belonged on Haverhill side, viz., Col. Charles Johnston and the Hon. James Woodward. The prospects of Haverhill were at that time very gloomy in respect to religion, and for nine months preceding the spring of 1790, there had not been a sermon preached in the place. But in the spring of that year, a melancholy death of a woman occurred in the house now occupied by Capt. Uriah Ward, which seemed to impress all minds with solemnity. She had lived far from righteousness, and died in great agony of soul in view of her endless ruin. And now the precious grain, sown by the Rev. Mr. Powers, which had lain buried long, being watered by the dews and rains of divine grace, and warmed by the vivifying rays of the Sun of righteousness, began to germinate and to appear, to the great joy of those few who had waited and prayed for consolation in Israel. The holy and blessed spirit seemed to come down upon them as a rushing, mighty wind; and it was but a short time before there was but one house, from the Dow farm to Piermont line, in which there was no special awakening with the occupants. That house was at the Ayers' place. In all other habitations there were wailings for sin. People pressed together for prayer and instruction, and clergymen, hearing of the wonders of God at Haverhill, came to obtain and to impart a blessing. The Rev. Dr. Burton, of Thetford, and Rev. Dr. Burroughs, of Hanover, were peculiarly helpful, and their labors are remembered with gratitude to this day by those who obtained the pearl of great price, and still survive. During that season, more than seventy persons became hopeful subjects of renewing grace. And although that church and people have witnessed repeated revivals of religion with them since that period, yet the elders among the people have never witnessed, as they think, the power of divine grace in equal degree. I have myself, while rejoicing with the newly converted in that place, and feeling that we witnessed great things, been reminded of the different feelings that were experienced by the Jews at Jerusalem, at the laying of the foundation of the second temple, on their return from captivity, when I heard the old saints speak of what they had witnessed. It will be recollected that the younger Jews, who had never seen the first temple, rejoiced greatly in the prospect of having a temple for worship. The older Jews rejoiced also ; but when they contrasted their then present circumstances with what they had been in the glory of the first temple, for a time grief preponderated in their breasts, and there was a mixed shout of joy and grief. So it has repeatedly been at Haverhill. The converts of 1790 have ever been disposed to meditate on the power of divine grace of that year ; and although they could rejoice in the day of small things, yet they have longed to see one more day *of the right hand of the Most High*.

On the 13th of October, 1790, the church was first organized. Rev. Dr. Burton, Rev. Dr. Burroughs, and Rev. Mr. Ward, of Plymouth, officiated. Twenty-two members constituted the church at its organization. Rev. Ethan Smith was their first pastor. He was ordained, January 25, 1792, and continued their pastor a little more than seven years ; dismissed June 23, 1799. The Rev. John Smith succeeded Mr. Ethan Smith, and was ordained, December 23, 1802, and continued their pastor a little more than four years ; dismissed, January 14, 1807. From this time to January 4, 1815, the church and ecclesiastical society had no pastor, nor had they uninterrupted preaching, but had many candidates and occasional preaching. And here we have a melancholy exhibition of the mutable state of every church on earth. The church that was so flourishing in 1792, was reduced in July, 1814, at the time when I commenced my labors among them, to twelve members in the south parish—three males, and nine females,—and a covering of sackcloth was spread upon the tent of Zion. But eight persons within the limits of the parish had made a public profession of religion for the last twenty-two years. Two were received under the Rev. Ethan Smith, from 1792 to 1799; two under the Rev. John Smith, from 1802 to 1807; and four under the Rev. David Sutherland, of Bath, their moderator, from 1807 to 1814. In the same time there were one hundred and eight baptisms, four of whom were adults.

In the autumn early of 1814, the people began again to flow together to hear the word of life, and a still, small voice was heard by many, saying, *This is the way—walk ye in it.* Many obeyed that voice. It was impressively true, that the Lord did not advance, in this instance, in a "great and strong wind," nor in the "earthquake," nor in the "fire;" but his coming was as the ushering in of day. The first evidence of the King's presence was seen in the profound stillness which reigned in the worshipping assembly, and the fixed attention of the hearer. Christians began to feel that they were newly anointed from on high, and they prayed with tenderness and fervor, and sinners would drop a tear, when pointedly addressed upon the concerns of their souls. Soon we were told that this one, and that one, were deeply anxious for their spiritual interest. And these instances were multiplied until very many were pricked in heart, and would inquire to know what they must do to be saved. In a short time, some began to rejoice in hope; and this solemn and joyful state of things continued through the remaining part of 1814, and more or less through 1815. On the 4th of January, 1815, I received ordination, and before the close of that year, I think, more than sixty were added to the church; some became *pillars*, and remain so to the present day, although some have fallen asleep.

In 1822, we were blessed with another revival, but not so extensive as the former. Some were called and added to the church in 1826; and at the close of my ministry in this place,—which occurred, April 28, 1829, nearly fifteen years after I came among them, —there had been added to the church one hundred and nineteen members. There had been one hundred and ninety-one baptisms, thirty-five of whom were adults.

The Rev. Henry Wood was installed their pastor, December 14, 1831, and was dismissed, March 3, 1835. The Rev. Joseph Gibbs was ordained their pastor, June 16, 1835, and departed this life, April 11, 1837. Rev. Archibald Fleming was installed, June 27, 1838, and still remains their pastor.

With my best wishes and my prayers for their mutual prosperity and final salvation, I close these Sketches.

Your much obliged and ever grateful friend,

GRANT POWERS.

APPENDIX.

The two following anecdotes were originally written for newspaper publication ; but the publishers of the Historical Collections of New Hampshire, learning through the late Jesse Worcester, Esq., of Hollis, the historical accuracy of the two pieces, in point of fact, adopted them both, as I have understood, into their Collections. But as comparatively few will ever read them in those Collections, and as the writer of the present Sketches was the author of those two communications, he feels that he has an undoubted right to append them to this work ; and when we consider the peculiar agency and interest the two individuals, who are the hero and heroine in the anecdotes, had in the discovery and the settlement of the Coos, we cannot but feel that our readers will be gratified in the perusal of those adventures. The writer often heard the aged widow of Capt. Powers relate the facts as here stated ; the language is, of course, his own.

THE BOAR AND THE BEAR.

The town of Hollis, in the county of Hillsborough, N. H., is one of the oldest towns in the county, and was first settled by Capt. Peter Powers, and Anna, his wife, from Hampshire, Dunstable, 1831. Those early settlers were accustomed to the rearing of many swine, by permitting them to run at large in the woods, and to subsist upon roots, acorns, and nuts, which were produced in great abundance in the place. In the fall of the year, or at the time of the first deep snow, the older members of the herd, that were originally tame, would lead their numerous progeny into winter quarters, at a shed erected for that purpose some distance from the house, where the owner disposed of them as he pleased, although many of them were as untame and as ferocious as the beasts of the mountains. At that time, bears were plenty, and very hostile to swine. It became necessary, therefore, to provide for the defence of the herd by permitting one of the males to live several years beyond the period of life ordinarily assigned to that species by man ; at which time he became literally the *master of the flock*. His tusks protruded on either side, in nearly semi-circles, to the distance of six or seven inches. He seemed conscious of his superiority and responsibility. He was fierce in the extreme, and courted danger ; and when the heard was assailed, he instantly presented himself to the foe, with eyes darting fire, with tusks heated to blueness, and foaming at the mouth in a terrific manner. He roamed the forest, unconscious of danger ; he led the herd ; and but few of the untamed tribes had the temerity to dispute his title to supremacy.

It happened, however, on a certain day in autumn, when Anna stood in the door of her cabin, listening to the oft-repeated sound of the descending axe, or the crash of falling trees, while her husband was at his daily task, that she heard from a great distance the faint, yet distinct, cry of one of their herd. She thought it was the cry of expiring nature. She remained in this state of suspense but a short time, before the heard came rushing from the forest in the greatest apparent trepidation. The oldest dams of the herd, much exhausted, and without their common leader and protector, seemed inclined to take refuge in the apartment which had been their retreat in former winters ; but the younger branches of the family would not follow them. The dams, seeing this, dashed on through the cleared space, and disappeared in the forest on the north side. The cries of the wounded were still heard, but grew fainter and fainter, until wholly lost in death. But the anxious Anna had not removed from her position, before the old boar came rushing through the bushes in eager pursuit of his charge, which had eloped and left him in the rear by many a rood. He was fresh from the field of combat. He was bathed in blood, foaming at the mouth, gnashing his tusks, and exhibited a terrific aspect. Regardless of home, he approached a field of corn which grew near the cabin, and leaped the fence, not touching the topmost knot, although it was proof against horses which strayed through the woods from neighboring towns in Massachusetts. He passed directly through the field without touching a kernel of corn, and leaping the fence on the opposite side, disappeared in the woods. Not long after, the wished-for husband, whose presence the gathering shades of evening, the deep solitude of the place, and the stirring events of the afternoon, had rendered peculiarly inviting to the young partner of his toils and hopes, returned with his axe upon his shoulder, enlivening the forest with his evening whistle, and driving his old bellcow before him, which summoned Anna with her milk-pail to her evening task.

Scarcely had he secured the topmost rail to his yard enclosure, when Anna from the window of her cabin saw her husband held in anxious suspense. For some moments he paused and listened ; but turned and called, "Anna, Anna, bring me my gun and ammunition in a minute, for the *Old Master* himself is worsted." They were at his hand in a trice. "Look to yourself," said the husband,* and bounded into the forest. Pursuing with great speed the course whence the sound proceeded, which alone broke the silence of the evening, our adventurer soon found himself at a distance of about a mile and a half from his cabin, surrounded with black alders, so thickly set as to be almost impenetrable to man and beast. Before him lay *Long Pond*, so called, about one mile in length, and from a quarter to a half a mile, perhaps, in width. He was near mid-way of the pond, and the sound from the laboring boar and his antagonist (a mixed, frightful yell) proceeded directly from the opposite shore. Nothing now remained but for him to plunge into the pond, and make the opposite shore by beating the waves, or to divide him a passage amidst the alders around one of the extremities of the pond, which could not be done short of travelling the distance of another mile. But no time was to be lost. The cries of the boar bespoke the greatest need, and the latter course was adopted ; and in a space of time, and with the courage and energy which are scarcely conceived by the present generation, he arrived at the scene of action. Whose heart does not now misgive him, while nearing the battle ground, alone, in darkness, and all uncertain as to the nature of the foe ? But young Powers advanced with undaunted firmness. He was

---

*Indians were then numerous in the town.

under the necessity of approaching near to the belligerents before he could make any discovery, by reason of the darkness of the night, rendered more dark by the towering trees, which mingled their branches at some sixty or seventy feet from the ground, and a dense underwood, which stood like a hedge continually before him. But as soon as he entered the area which had been beaten down during the action, he discovered the boar seated upon the ground, and still defending himself against the furious assaults of the hugest bear his eyes ever beheld! She was like his old *bell-cow* for magnitude! He drew his gun to an *aim*, when he perceived, obscurely, that the bear was on a line with him and his hog, and he could not discharge his piece without putting the life of the latter in jeopardy; and, as he was moving in a circular direction, to procure a safe discharge, he was discovered by the bear, and she bounded into the bushes. Powers now came up to the boar, and witnessed such tokens of gladness as surprised him. It was, however, too solemn an hour with the swine to lavish upon his deliverer unmeaning ceremonies. As soon as he found himself released from his too powerful antagonist, he prostrated himself upon the ground, and lay some time, panting and groaning in a manner truly affecting to his owner. Powers now discharged his gun, with a view to terrify the beasts of prey, and keep them off during the night. He struck and kindled a fire, and upon a slight examination, he found that his hog was lacerated in his rear in a shocking manner. He was utterly disabled from rising except upon his fore feet. But to show the indomitable nature of the animal, I will relate that the boar, after some little time, recovered in a degree from his extreme exhaustion, and gaining the same position he had when his owner found him, began to beat a challenge for a renewal of the combat. Again his eyes flashed with rage, he stamped with his fore feet, he chafed, gnashed with his tusks, and foaming at the mouth, he looked around with the greatest apparent firmness for his antagonist. Our adventurer now drew together fallen wood sufficient to support a fire through the night, burnt powder around his swine, and returned to his cabin, where he was never more joyfully received by the young wife, who, during all this while, had remained listening at the window in painful solicitude.

The next day, some help was obtained, as one family* had, prior to this, moved in and settled in the south-west part of the town, and the battle ground was revisited. The boar had not moved out of his place, but was still weltering in his blood. With much labor he was conveyed home in a cart, and, as he never could become the defence of the herd again, he was yarded, fattened, and killed, and helped by his death to promote that existence to the family which he could no longer do by his life.

With a view to account for the melancholy fate of the boar, Powers and his associates went in search of the swine that was destroyed in the afternoon of the preceding day. They found one of their largest hogs slain by a bear, and, near to, a large bear was as evidently slain by the boar. From this they inferred that the first hog was mortally wounded by a bear in the absence of the boar ; but the cries of the wounded soon brought the *Master*, when a battle ensued, in which the bear was slain, not, however, without loss of blood with the boar ; that during this first action, the rest of the herd fled, and that the boar was in pursuit of them when he passed the cabin through the field ; that after running some miles, at the point of exhaustion, he fell in with a still more powerful antagonist, when his fight was comparatively feeble, and he fell *overpowered*, but not *subdued*, as it has fallen out with many a Greek and Roman hero.

AN ADVENTUROUS VISIT.

When Capt. Peter Powers and Anna, his wife, first pitched their tent in Hollis, 1731, which was a little north-west of the present meeting-house, the traces of which are still visible, their nearest neighbor lived in the south-eastern part of Dunstable, N. H., a distance, probably, at this time, of ten miles, and could not be made at that period at a less travelling distance than twelve miles, as they had no road but a single track, and spotted trees for their guide.

---

*Eleazer Flagg.

This journey could not be made in the summer season without fording the Nashua, which was done a little southeast of a small island, visible at your left, as you now pass the bridge, going from Hollis, N. H., to Dunstable, Mass.; and here the river was fordable only when the streams were low. Of course, these lonely adventurers made their visits but seldom, and never with a view to be absent from their habitation during the night, as they were then the parents of two children, whom they were necessitated to leave at home, in a cabin surrounded by Indians. Indeed, never did both parents leave their children and perform this route in company.

Now, it happened on a summer's morning, in the month of August, that the wife, Anna, found it convenient to visit her *neighbor*, and mounting at an early hour a fine Narraganset, a faithful and tried companion in adventures, the river was soon forded, and the whole distance was made, long ere it was high noon. The interview was such as characterized the first settlers in this new country, where warmth of affection more than supplied the place of a thousand ceremonies, and a sense of dependence promoted to the discharge of kinder offices than mere refinement would recognize as obligatory on her.

The hours passed swiftly away—they lived fast—they ate, they drank, they talked much, and blessed God and their king. Nor did a single occurrence tend to interrupt their festivity until about three past meridian, when all were suddenly aroused by a distant, though heavy, discharge of heaven's artillery. All rushed to the door to witness the aspect of the elements, when, lo ! it was most threatening and appalling ! Nature all around slept, or seemed to be awed into a deathlike silence. Not a leaf moved but when the foundations of the earth responded to the voice of heaven. Already, from north to south, the whole western horizon was mantled in black, and the gathering tempest moved forward as slowly and sublimely as though conscious of its power to deride all resistance ! Not until this moment did anxious concern possess the breast of Anna for the objects of her affections, whom she had left in that lone, dear cell. In a kind of momentary distraction, she demanded that Narraganset should be pannelled, for she must return to her family that afternoon, whatever might be the consequence to herself. She had rather brave the tempest returning, than endure her forebodings with her sheltered friends. But a sudden change in the elements, did more to dissuade her from so rash an attempt than the entreaties and expostulation of her friends. From an apparent calm, nature now awoke and seemed to be rushing into ruin. As though the north called unto the south, and the west unto the east, the four winds came on to the conflict. Clouds were driven hither and thither in angry velocity and all seemed to be propelled in directions counter to each other. The tempest soon burst upon them, and on the whole adjacent country, in an unparalleled torrent. Nothing was heard but the crack or roll of thunder, and the roar of winds and waters—nothing seen but the successive blaze of lightning!

"Intonuere poli, et crebris micat ignibus æther."

The said Anna lived until rising somewhat of ninety years, and could remember distinctly more than eighty years ; but, in all this time, she never witnessed such a scene, nor could she relate any thing which seemed to raise such sublimity of feeling in her mind as this.

The tempest lay upon them with unabated force several hours, nor did it appear to spend itself until the sun was just sinking below the horizon, when it broke in upon drowned nature in all its smiles, and reflected its golden beams upon the black cloud at the east, in the most enchanting manner. This was the moment for Anna to renew her resolve of returning to her family that night ; and, contrary to all reasoning and persuasions, she instantly put it in execution. She mounted her horse, and bidding adieu to her friends, she entered the twelve-mile forest just as the sun took his leave of her. She calculated upon a serene and starlight evening, and the extraordinary instinct of her beast, as well as her experience in the way and at the fords. But in regard to the former, she was wholly disappointed. The wind soon shifted, and rolled the same cloud back again ; the rain recommenced as the night set in, and the wind ceased.

At that season of the year, the time of twilight was short ; the earth being warmed and moistened, evaporation was rapid, and a dense fog arose, which soon obstructed vision, and, long ere she arrived at the fords, she was enveloped in total darkness. Her only guide now was her faithful Narraganset, and the beasts of the forest her companions. She, however, made the best of her circumstances. She entered into conversation with her mare, as was her custom when riding alone ; and when her beast stopped suddenly and tossed up her head, and snorted at some wild animal crossing her track, as was supposed, Anna would exhort her to possess courage, assuring her "that nothing could harm her, for the beasts were mere cowards in the presence of a brave horse," &c.

After this manner, the long way to the fords was passed over in Egyptian darkness ; nor had the thought once occurred to Anna that so considerable a river as now rolled before her would be materially affected by a thunder storm of a few hours ; whereas, so great was the fall of water in this time that the river, although wide at this place, was bank full, and swept on with great rapidity. Nor could the rushing of the waters be heard by reason of the rain still pouring upon the forest around her. She therefore determined to give the rein to her experienced beast, believing that she would keep the ford, and land her on the opposite shore at the proper place. The horse entered the stream as soon as at the bank, and in a moment lost her foot-hold on terra firma, and was plunging in the waves at a full swim. Such, however, was Anna's presence of mind, that she made no exertion to rein her beast, but endeavored simply to retain her seat, which was now under water, whilst the waves beat against her waist. The faithful animal made for the opposite shore ; but so strong was the current, that she was either carried below the ford, or, in her exertions to resist it, she overacted and went above it, where, at one sweep of her fore feet, she struck upon a rock in the bed of the river, which suddenly raised her somewhat from the water forward ; but she as soon plunged again, for the rock was cleared the second sweep. This plunge was so deep that Anna was borne from her pannel by the gravity of the water, but pitching forward, she seized Narraganset's mane as she rose, nor did she quit her grasp, until they were both safely landed on the happy shore ! adjusting her clothes, she remounted, and soon found that her beast was in her accustomed track, and, in little more than one hour, she alighted at the door of her peaceful cabin, where, by her well-known signal,* she broke the slumber of her husband and babes, and on entering related, in no purer gratitude or greater joy than they experienced in hearing, the result of that adventurous night.

---

* Capt. Powers and wife agreed on a peculiar rap, which served as a kind of countersign to inform the one within that the other had arrived and desired admission. This was necessary to prevent the intrusion of Indians, who would often rap at different hours of the night.

DEED OF THE COOS COUNTRY.

To all persons to whom these Presents shall come, Greeting :

Know ye, that I Philip, an Indian, a native of America now resident in upper Coos & Chief thereof,

For & in consideration of the sum hereafter named for which I have received security to my full satisfaction of Thomas Eames of Northumberland in the County of Grafton & State of New Hampshire & his associates namely, John Bradley & Jonathan Eastman of Concord, county of Rockingham & Nathan Hoit of Moultonborough in the County of Strafford all in the state of New Hampshire Esqrs, all my peculiar friends. I this day have given, bargained sold, released, conveyed & confirmed & by these presents do give, grant, bargain, sell, convey & confirm to them the said Thomas, John, Jonathan & Nathan their heirs & assigns forever all that tract or parcel of land & waters situate within the following boundaries, Viz, Beginning on the East side of Conneetteecook now called Connecticut River at the mouth of Ammanoosuck River, then up said Ammanoosuck river to Head Pond to the carrying place, then across the carrying place to a small pond on the head of Peumpelussuck or dead river, then down said river to Andrewscoggin river, then up Andrewscoggin River to the Lake Hambagog, including all the waters of said Lake & Islands from said lake up Andrewscoggin River to Allogunanabagogg Lake, including all the waters & Islands in said Lake, then up said Andrewscoggin River to Molleychungomuck Lake, thence along the easterly side of said Lake to the outlet of Mooselukmegantick, then up said river to said Lake Mooseluckmegantick including all the waters & Islands thereof, then across the carrying place Quasuktecuck, thence down said river till it empties into Awsisgowassuck River, then up said river to Palmachinanabagogg Lake including all the waters & Islands thereof, thence up Awsisgowassuck River to the carrying place that leads into Awseecunticook River or St. Frances River, thence down said river till it falls into the branch which empties from Lake Mamsloobagogg, then up said River to Skessawannoock Lake, thence up said River to said Mamsloobagogg, including all the waters & Islands thereof, from thence up Masskeecoowanggawnall River to the head thereof, then across the carrying place to the head of Nulpeagawnuck, then down said river to Conneeteecook or Connecticut river then down said river including all the Islands thereof to the mouth of Ammunoosuck river, the place began at, agreeably to a plan I have this day given to them, their heirs & assigns forever with the following conditions & reservations, namely that I reserve free liberty to hunt all sorts of wild game on any of the foregoing territories, and taking fish in any of the waters thereof for myself my heirs & *sucksessors* & all Indian tribes forever, also liberty of planting four bushels of corn & beans ; & this my trusty friend Thomas having given me security to furnish me & my Squaw with provisions & suitable clothing which I have accepted in full. I have for myself & in behalf of all Indians who hunted on or inhabited any of the foregoing lands or waters, forever quitclaimed & sold as aforesaid to them the said Thomas, John, Jonathan & Nathan as a good estate in fee simple, and do covenant with them that myself & my ancient Fathers forever & at all times have been in possession of the above described premises, & that I have a good right to & will warrant & defend the same to them the said Thomas, John, Jonathan & Nathan their heirs and assigns forever against the claims of all or any persons whatever.—In Witness whereof I have hereunto set my hand, seal & *signeture*, this twenty eighth day of June 1796.

     PHILIP + INDIAN CHIEF. [SEAL.]
        his / mark

     MOLLEY + MESSELL. [SEAL.]
        her / mark

     MOOSELECK + SUSSOP. [SEAL.]
        her / mark

Signed Sealed & Dld
 in presence of
  Ely Buel
  Jerem[b] Eames.

State of New Hampshire. Grafton, ss. June 30th, 1796.
Personally appeared Philip Indian Chief, Molley Messell & Mooseleck & acknowledged the foregoing instrument by them respectively subscribed to be their voluntary act & deed.
Before me
JERH EAMES, *Justice Peace.*

GRAFTON, SS. Nov. 22, 1796.
Received, Recorded & examined.
Attest,
JOHN ROGERS, *Regr.*

State of New Hampshire,
GRAFTON, SS. December 9, 1879.
I, Charles H. Day, Register of Deeds, for the County of Grafton, hereby certify that the foregoing is a true copy of Grafton County Records, Libro 23, Folio 206.
Attest,
C. H. DAY, *Reg. Deeds.*

INDEX.

Bailey, Gen. Jacob 35, 53
    190, 213—218
Bailey, Col Joshua..........50
Baker's River.........171—174
Barnes, J., lost son........171
Bradford, Vt...............160
Brook, Poole................46
Brown, Josiah.............170
Burton, D. D., Rev. Asa....83
    134—141, 154—158, 159
Campton 169
Cart with two tongues.....218
Chamberlain, John...141—142
Charters....................47
Claremont 129
Connel, John Mc......113—116
Cornish....................129
Cow, instinct of a..........89
Crank, saw-mill.........68—72
Dearborn, Samuel....165—171
Eastman, Amos............14
Elkins, Col. Jonathan......191
    197, 217
Elkins, Dea. Jonathan......52
Fairlee, East...............159
Fifield's, A., lost son.......164
Flood......................110
Freeman, Col. Otis 78
Foreman, John..............50
Groton.....................169

Hanover ......78—80, 130—133
Harriman, Polly............46
Hazen, Capt. John.......36, 43
Hebron 169
Hobart, Capt. James..... 165
Holderness 169
Howard, Col. Joshua.......43
Howard, Deacon........80—82
Hughs, John................43
Indians ....172—186
Instinct of a cow...........89
Johnston, Capt. Michael....45
Johnston, Col. Charles......45
    91, 95—103
Johnston, Michael....36, 40, 44
Johnson, Col. Thomas..47, 177
    190, 217
Kent, Col. Jacob............49
Kent, Mary 49
Ladd, Hon. Ezekiel.........52
Ladd, Mrs. Ruth 60, 67
Lancaster..................48
Lebanon 129
Living and Dress......119—120
Lyme... 130
Mann, Esq., John.....124—128
Morse, Uriah 46
Norwich, Vt..........134—144
Orford....................126
Osmer, John....... ..160—163

Ox Bow, Great, old Indian Settlement............36—39
Page, John............49, 69, 71
Parker, Lieut. Z............165
Peabody, Nathaniel........209
Peters, Esq., Andrew B....162
Pettie, John..........36, 40, 44
Piermont ....119—120
Pigeons....................109
Plainfield 129
Plymouth........165, 168—175
Plymouth, first ox-team from.....................116
Powers, Capt. Peter,....15—32, 84—87
Powers, Rev. Peter.....53—57, 75—88
Revivals...............219—221
Rogers, Col. Robert ....34—35
Rumney....................169
Sleeper, Samuel.....40, 61—63
Sparks, Jared..............211
Stark, Gen. John ......13—14
Strong, Joel................157

Thanksgiving 74
Thetford, Vt.........141—159
Thornton...................169
Tyler, Jonathan......120—12.
Wait's River...............163
Walbridge..............78—80
Wallace, Mrs..........146—148
Wallace, Richard ....91—94, 113—118, 143—153
Warren 169
Washington, Gen.....202—212
Ward, Rev. Nathan...166—168
Way, Mr 56, 57
Weare, Meshech...........208
Webster, Ephraim....150—154
Webster, Lydia............168
Wentworth, ...169
Wheeler, Charles..........181
Wheeler, Glazier, ...40, 44
Willard, Oliver..........41, 42
Woodward, Hon. James....48, 64—71
Worms...............103—108
Wright, Benoni..........62, 63

www.ingramcontent.com/pod-product-compliance
Lightning Source LLC
Chambersburg PA
CBHW022007220426
43663CB00007B/1000